2 dos

¡Avancemos!

Lecturas para TODOS
with TEST PREPARATION

HOLT McDOUGAL
a division of Houghton Mifflin Harcourt

Acknowledgments

"Oda al aceite," from *Odas elementales* by Pablo Neruda. Fundación Pablo Neruda, 1954. Reprinted with the permission of Agencia Literaria Carmen Balcells, S.A., Barcelona, Spain.

"Oda a la sal," from *Odas elementales* by Pablo Neruda. Fundación Pablo Neruda, 1954. Reprinted with the permission of Agencia Literaria Carmen Balcells, S.A., Barcelona, Spain.

Isabel Allende, an excerpt from the work, *La casa de los espíritus* by Isabel Allende. © Isabel Allende, 1982. Reprinted by permission of Agencia Literaria Carmen Balcells, S.A.

From *Senderos fronterizos* by Francisco Jiménez. Spanish translation copyright © 2002 by Francisco Jiménez. Copyright © 2001 by Francisco Jiménez. Reprinted with permission from the author.

From *Escrituras: Frida Kahlo* by Raquel Tibol. DR © 2001, Universidad Nacional Autónoma de México. DR © 2001, Consejo Nacional para la Cultura y las Artes. Reprinted by permission of Universidad Nacional Autónoma de México.

"A Julia de Burgos," from *Song of the Simple Truth* by Julia de Burgos. Copyright © Julia de Burgos. Reprinted by permission of Curbstone Press.

From *Platero y yo* by Juan Ramón Jiménez. © Herederos de Juan Ramón Jiménez. Reprinted by permission.

From *El delantal blanco* by Sergio Vodanovic. © Herederos de Sergio Vodanovic. © Pehuen Editores, 1990. Reprinted by permission.

Isabel Allende, an excerpt from the work, *La casa de los espíritus* by Isabel Allende. Copyright © Isabel Allende, 1982. Reprinted by permission of Agencia Literaria Carmen Balcells, S.A.

Illustration and **Photography Credits** appear on page 228.

ISBN-13: 978-0-618-76604-8
ISBN-10: 0-618-76604-9   5 6 7 8 9 – 0956 – 12 11 10 09
Internet: www.holtmcdougal.com

Contents

Literatura adicional

Academic and Informational Reading

Test Preparation Strategies

Welcome to *Lecturas para todos*

Reading Skills Improvement— in Spanish *and* English

You will read selections from your Spanish textbook as well as readings from great Spanish-language literature. Materials in English will help you practice understanding the types of texts you encounter in school, on tests, and in the real world. As you work with all the selections, you will find your reading skills in both languages improving!

At the end of the book, you will also study and practice strategies for taking standardized tests.

Lecturas culturales and *Literatura adicional*

These readings from your textbook and from Spanish-language literature will give you a chance to improve your reading skills and Spanish vocabulary. You will also gain invaluable cultural insights and have the opportunity to experience literature.

Before You Read

Before each reading, the *Para leer* page prepares you with features to help you anticipate the content of the reading.

Reading Strategy The strategy and graphic organizer allow you to decide how you will approach the material and to jot down your thoughts.

What You Need to Know This section tells you what to expect before you begin reading and gives you extra insights to help you get the most out of each selection.

While You Read

Point-of-use features next to the selections help you get the most out of each reading and make it your own.

Reading Tip For each selection, you will find a handy, specific reading tip to help with difficult or specialized language.

Lecturas para todos is a hands-on reading text that lets you take notes, highlight, underline text, and organize your thoughts on paper, so that you can master each reading and make it your own. The unique features of *Lecturas para todos* will help you quickly become comfortable with reading in Spanish and sharpen your comprehension skills both in Spanish and English.

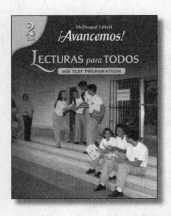

Links to ¡Avancemos!

When using McDougal Littell's *¡Avancemos!,* you will find *Lecturas para todos* to be a perfect companion. *Lecturas para todos* lets you mark up the *Lectura cultural* selections as you read, helping you understand and remember more.

Read on to learn more!

A pensar... These critical-thinking questions will help you analyze content as you read.

Márcalo This hands-on feature invites you to mark up the text by underlining and circling words and phrases right on the page.

> *Gramática* Highlighting key grammar concepts will help you reinforce and internalize them.
>
> *Vocabulario* Marking new vocabulary words in the text lets you practice them and see how they are used in natural contexts.
>
> *Análisis* This feature appears in the *Literatura adicional* section and encourages you to focus on one aspect of literary analysis as you read.

Reader's Success Strategy These notes give useful and fun tips and strategies for comprehending the selection.

Challenge These activities keep you challenged, even after you have grasped the basic concepts of the reading.

Vocabulary Support

Palabras clave Words that are important to understanding the readings appear in bold. The definitions appear at the bottom of each page.

After You Read

After you have read each selection, you will have the opportunity to practice key vocabulary, check your comprehension, and relate the reading to your own interests and experiences.

Vocabulario de la lectura A list of the *palabras clave* and their definitions is followed by two activities to help you practice these important words.

¿Comprendiste? Questions after each selection check your understanding of what you have read.

Conexión personal These short writing activities ask you to relate the selection to your life and experiences, making what you have read more meaningful to you.

Academic and Informational Reading

Here is a special collection of real-world examples—in English—to help you read every kind of informational material, from textbooks to technical directions. Why are these sections in English? Because the strategies you learn will help you on tests, in other classes, and in the world outside of school. You will find strategies for the following:

Analyzing Text Features This section will help you read many different types of magazine articles and textbooks. You will learn how titles, subtitles, lists, graphics, many different kinds of visuals, and other special features work in magazines and textbooks. After studying this section you will be ready to read even the most complex material.

Understanding Visuals Tables, charts, graphs, maps, and diagrams all require special reading skills. As you learn the common elements of various visual texts, you will learn to read these materials with accuracy and skill.

Recognizing Text Structures Informational texts can be organized in many different ways. In this section you will study the following structures and learn about special key words that will help you identify the organizational patterns:
• Main Idea and Supporting Details
• Problem and Solution
• Sequence
• Cause and Effect
• Comparison and Contrast
• Persuasion

Reading in the Content Areas You will learn special strategies for reading social studies, science, and mathematics texts.

Reading Beyond the Classroom In this section you will encounter applications, schedules, technical directions, product information, Web pages, and other readings. Learning to analyze these texts will help you in your everyday life and on some standardized tests.

Test Preparation Strategies

In this section, you will find strategies and practice to help you succeed on many different kinds of standardized tests. After closely studying a variety of test formats through annotated examples, you will have an opportunity to practice each format on your own. Additional support will help you think through your answers. You will find strategies for the following:

Successful Test Taking This section provides many suggestions for preparing for and taking tests. The information ranges from analyzing test questions to tips for answering multiple-choice and open-ended test questions.

Reading Tests: Long Selections You will learn how to analyze the structure of a lengthy reading and prepare to answer the comprehension questions that follow it.

Reading Tests: Short Selections These selections may be a few paragraphs of text, a poem, a chart or graph, or some other item. You will practice the special range of comprehension skills required for these pieces.

Functional Reading Tests These real-world texts present special challenges. You will learn about the various test formats that use applications, product labels, technical directions, Web pages, and more.

Revising-and-Editing Tests These materials test your understanding of English grammar and usage. You may encounter capitalization and punctuation questions. Sometimes the focus is on usage questions such as verb tenses or pronoun agreement issues. You will become familiar with these formats through the guided practice in this section.

Writing Tests Writing prompts and sample student essays will help you understand how to analyze a prompt and what elements make a successful written response. Scoring rubrics and a prompt for practice will prepare you for the writing tests you will take.

Lecturas culturales

Point-of-use comprehension support helps you read selections from *¡Avancemos!* and develop critical-thinking skills.

Para leer   *Vivir de la tierra*

Reading Strategy

USE WORD FAMILIES Guess the meaning of at least five new words based on "word families." For example, *cafetero* is in the same word family as *café*. Complete the table showing the familiar word, the new word, and its meaning.

Palabra que ya sé	Palabra nueva	Definición
café	cafetero	

What You Need to Know

Much of central Argentina is covered by the Pampas, a vast, flat, plain. This fertile land produces many of the country's agricultural crops and is home to Argentina's legendary cowboys, the *gauchos*. The number of *gauchos* has diminished in recent years as young people move to the cities, but many cattlemen are proud to preserve this lifestyle.

In the mountains of Colombia, coffee growing is a key industry. Coffee was first discovered in Eastern Africa. In time, its use spread to Turkey. In the 1700s, a French captain brought a coffee plant to the Caribbean island of Martinique. Coffee eventually made its way to the rest of tropical South and Central America.

Unidad 2, Lección 2
Vivir de la tierra   17

Reading Strategy
Reading tips and strategies give you a game plan for approaching the material and making sense of what you read.

What You Need to Know
Additional information and background provide you with a key to unlock the selection so that you can better understand and enjoy it.

Lecturas culturales continued

READING TIP
Help with difficult or specialized language lowers the barriers to comprehension.

READER'S SUCCESS STRATEGY
These strategies offer suggestions to help you read the selection successfully. Sometimes you will have a chart to fill in while you read; other times you will find ideas for mentally organizing the information you find.

CHALLENGE
This feature asks you to expand upon what you have learned from the reading and think more deeply about the themes and ideas it contains.

READING TIP ¿Look at the words that are surrounded by **comillas** («»). These function in the same way as quotation marks in English.

READER'S SUCCESS STRATEGY In order to improve your reading, you might want to read this passage several times silently. Rereading helps you improve fluency. As you practice rereading, you will recognize common words more quickly, you will group similar words together to make meaning clearer, and you will even increase your reading rate.

CHALLENGE What point does this reading make about the lives of the **gauchos** and **cafeteros**? State the main idea in a sentence. Then write at least three details that support the main idea. **(Identify Main Ideas and Details)**

1. _____

2. _____

3. _____

18   Lecturas para todos

Vivir de la tierra

Un gaucho argentino en ropa tradicional

La vida[1] del gaucho es la vida de un **ganadero** que vive de **la tierra**. La región del gaucho es
5   La Pampa, tierra de mucho sol y de **llanos**. Estas condiciones determinan lo que hace el gaucho día a día.
10 Los gauchos se levantan **temprano** para atender el ganado[2] y para mantener los ranchos. El «**sueldo**» del gaucho es la carne y la piel del ganado que vende.

Estas condiciones también definen qué
15 ropa se pone y qué comida comen él y su familia regularmente. Para trabajar, se pone un sombrero grande para protegerse del sol, del viento y de la **lluvia**. Se pone pantalones que se llaman «bombachas» y unas botas
20 altas. En la casa del gaucho comen lo que

[1] life   [2] cattle

Las pampas de Argentina, la tierra del gaucho

PALABRAS CLAVE
el ganadero   *cattle rancher*
la tierra   *land, soil*
el llano   *prairie*

temprano   *early*
el sueldo   *salary*
la lluvia   *rain*

Level 2

---

produce el gaucho: por ejemplo, el asado—
una variedad de carnes— es el plato típico de
los gauchos.

Las montañas[3] de Colombia son ideales
25 para el cultivo del café: son húmedas, altas
y **frescas**. En Colombia, el café es muy
importante. Hay una «cultura del café». El
café colombiano es famoso también en otros
países: es uno de los mejores del mundo[4].

30 El cafetero colombiano debe trabajar la
tierra constantemente. ¿Cómo es un día típico
de un cafetero? Los cafeteros se acuestan
temprano y se levantan muy temprano todos
los días. Normalmente se despiertan entre
35 las dos y las cuatro de la mañana. Se arreglan
para salir: se ponen la ruana, o poncho, y
el sombrero grande. Algunos todavía van
en mula[5] a su trabajo, una tradición de los
cafeteros. Van a los campos todos los días para
40 cultivar y mantener[6] el café. Más tarde, deben
sacar los granos de café[7] porque luego tienen
que prepararlos para convertirlos en la famosa
bebida.

---

[3] mountains   [4] world   [5] mule
[6] maintain   [7] **granos**... coffee beans

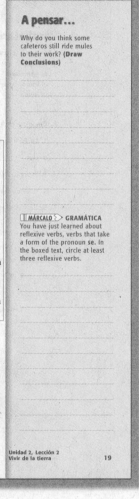

*Un cafetero
colombiano
saca los granos
de café.*

Cultivos de café, cerca de Armenia, Colombia

PALABRAS CLAVE
fresco(a) *cool*

A pensar...

Why do you think some
cafeteros still ride mules
to their work? **(Draw
Conclusions)**

▦ MÁRCALO ◈ **GRAMÁTICA**
You have just learned about
reflexive verbs, verbs that take
a form of the pronoun **se**. In
the boxed text, circle at least
three reflexive verbs.

Unidad 2, Lección 2
Vivir de la tierra   19

A pensar...

Point-of-use questions check
your understanding and ask
you to think critically about the
passage.

▦ MÁRCALO ◈ **GRAMÁTICA**
This feature assists you with
the new grammar as you read
the selection. Underlining or
circling the examples helps you
internalize and remember the
grammar.

PALABRAS CLAVE
Important vocabulary words
appear in bold within the
reading. Definitions are given
at the bottom of the page.

Lecturas culturales   *continued*

Vocabulario de la lectura
Vocabulary practice follows each reading, reinforcing the *palabras clave* that appear throughout the selection. Words that appear in blue are lesson vocabulary words in *¡Avancemos!*

Vocabulario de la lectura

Palabras clave

fresco(a)   *cool*
el ganadero   *cattle rancher*
el llano   *prairie*
la lluvia   *rain*

el sueldo   *salary*
temprano   *early*
la tierra   *land, soil*

A. Complete each sentence by writing one of the **Palabras clave** in the blank.

1. La Pampa es la _____ de los gauchos.

2. Los _____ de las Pampas son todos iguales, sin altos ni bajos.

3. Los gauchos y los cafeteros se despiertan _____.

4. Cuando hace _____ me pongo un suéter.

5. Con el sombrero se protege del agua de la _____.

B. Find the synonym for each **Palabra clave**. Write the letter for the synonym in the blank.

_____ **1.** el ganadero   a. precipitación

_____ **2.** el sueldo   b. ranchero

_____ **3.** la lluvia   c. un poco frío

_____ **4.** fresco(a)   d. salario

¿Comprendiste?

¿Comprendiste?
Comprehension questions
check your understanding and
provide the opportunity to
practice new vocabulary words.

¿Comprendiste?

1. ¿Cómo se llama la región de Argentina donde viven los gauchos?

_____

2. ¿Cuáles son las actividades del gaucho? ¿Qué produce el gaucho? ¿El cafetero?

_____

3. ¿Qué se pone un gaucho para trabajar? ¿Un cafetero?

_____
_____

4. Compara la rutina diaria del gaucho con la rutina del cafetero. ¿A qué hora se levantan? ¿Qué se ponen?

_____
_____
_____

Conexión personal

Look at the daily routine of the *gaucho* and the coffee grower, and write their activities in the chart below. Then write your own daily activities. How might your day be more interesting than that of a *gaucho* or *cafetero,* or why might it be more boring? Use details from the chart to explain your reasons.

LA RUTINA DIARIA

El gaucho	El cafetero	Yo

Conexión personal
These short writing activities
will help you connect the
information and events in the
selections with your own life
and interests.

Literatura adicional

Notes in the margins make literature from the Spanish-speaking world accessible and help you read works by famous authors such as Pablo Neruda.

Reading Strategy
This feature provides reading tips and strategies that help you effectively approach the material.

What You Need to Know
This section provides a key to help you unlock the selection so that you can understand and enjoy it.

LITERATURA ADICIONAL

Para leer   *La casa de los espíritus*

Reading Strategy

UNDERSTAND CHARACTERS' MOTIVES Motives are the emotions, wants, or needs that cause a character to act or react in a certain way. As you read this excerpt from *La casa de los espíritus*, use the chart below to understand the actions of the main characters. Next to each action, describe the reason, or motivation, the character had for taking it.

Acción	Razón
1. Esteban Trueba pide ser recibido en la casa de la familia del Valle.	
2. Esteban pide autorización para visitar a Clara del Valle de nuevo.	
3. Clara le pregunta a Esteban si él quiere casarse con ella.	
4. Clara está dispuesta a casarse con Esteban.	

What You Need to Know

This reading in an excerpt from the novel *La casa de los espíritus (The House of the Spirits)* by Chilean writer Isabel Allende. It was originally published in Spain in 1982. The novel narrates the history of several generations of the Trueba family in Chile. Esteban Trueba had been in love with and engaged to marry Rosa, the oldest daughter of the del Valle family. The youngest daughter, Clara, is clairvoyant and announced that there would be a death in the house. Rosa died shortly afterward, and Clara didn't speak again for nine years. Her silence was broken on her nineteenth birthday with the announcement that she was going to marry Rosa's fiancé. Two months later, Esteban Trueba appears.

Level 2

Level 2

LITERATURA ADICIONAL

READING TIP Poems often contain repeated elements and patterns. Look for repetition and patterns as you read the poem. Note that the indented words are part of the previous line.

APUNTES

CHALLENGE Read the boxed text. What do you think Julia de Burgos means? (**Analyze**)

MÁRCALO ANÁLISIS
Antithesis is the contrast of a word, phrase, or idea against another with the opposite meaning. **Mentira** and **verdad** are an example. Find and circle other uses of antithesis in the poem. Write the pairs of words on the lines below.

Sobre la autora

Julia de Burgos nació en Carolina (Bayamón), Puerto Rico, en 1914, siendo la mayor de trece hermanos. Escritora y poeta, es casi una leyenda en Puerto Rico. Después de vivir en zonas provincianas de Puerto Rico, se mudó a Cuba y luego a Nueva York. Publicó sólo dos libros durante su vida: *Poemas en 20 surcos* (1938) y *Canción de la verdad sencilla* (1939). Murió en Nueva York en 1953. Su libro *El mar y tú* se publicó un año después de su muerte.

A Julia de Burgos

Ya las gentes murmuran que yo soy tu
    enemiga
porque dicen que en verso doy al mundo
    tu yo.

5 **Mienten,** Julia de Burgos. Mienten,
    Julia de Burgos.

La que se alza[1] en mis versos no es tu voz:
    es mi voz
porque tú eres **ropaje** y la esencia soy yo;
10 y el más profundo abismo se tiende[2] entre
    las dos.

Tú eres fría muñeca de mentira social,
y yo, viril destello[3] de la humana verdad.

Tú, **miel** de cortesanas[4] hipocresías; yo no;
15 que en todos mis poemas desnudo[5] el corazón.

[1] rises   [2] stretches out, spreads   [3] flash, glimmer   [4] courtly
[5] I lay bare

PALABRAS CLAVE
mentir *to lie*   **la miel** *honey*
el ropaje *vestment*

Sobre la autora
Each literary selection begins with a short author biography that provides cultural context.

READING TIPS
These tips help you approach the selection and understand points where language or structure is difficult.

CHALLENGE
These activities keep you challenged, even after you have grasped the basic concepts of the reading.

MÁRCALO ANÁLISIS
This feature encourages you to focus on one aspect of literary analysis as you read.

Academic and Informational Reading

This section helps you read informational material and prepare for other classes and standardized tests.

VARIED TYPES OF READINGS

The wide variety of academic and informational selections helps you access different types of readings and develop specific techniques for those reading types.

Academic and Informational Reading

In this section you'll find strategies to help you read all kinds of informational materials. The examples here range from magazines you read for fun to textbooks to schedules. Applying these simple and effective techniques will help you be a successful reader of the many texts you encounter every day.

143

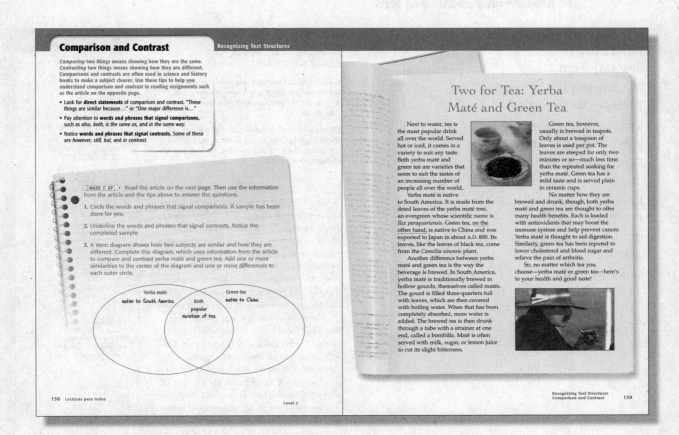

Comparison and Contrast

Comparing two things means showing how they are the same. *Contrasting* two things means showing how they are different. Comparisons and contrasts are often used in science and history books to make a subject clearer. Use these tips to help you understand comparison and contrast in reading assignments such as the article on the opposite page.

• Look for **direct statements** of comparison and contrast. "These things are similar because…" or "One major difference is…"

• Pay attention to **words and phrases that signal comparisons**, such as *also, both, is the same as,* and *in the same way.*

• Notice **words and phrases that signal contrasts.** Some of these are *however, still, but,* and *in contrast.*

MARK IT UP Read the article on the next page. Then use the information from the article and the tips above to answer the questions.

1. Circle the words and phrases that signal comparisons. A sample has been done for you.

2. Underline the words and phrases that signal contrasts. Notice the completed sample.

3. A Venn diagram shows how two subjects are similar and how they are different. Complete this diagram, which uses information from the article to compare and contrast yerba maté and green tea. Add one or more similarities to the center of the diagram and one or more differences to each outer circle.

Yerba maté — native to South America
Both — popular varieties of tea
Green tea — native to China

158 Lecturas para todos

Level 2

Two for Tea: Yerba Maté and Green Tea

Next to water, tea is the most popular drink all over the world. Served hot or iced, it comes in a variety to suit any taste. Both yerba maté and green tea are varieties that seem to suit the tastes of an increasing number of people all over the world.

Yerba maté is native to South America. It is made from the dried leaves of the yerba maté tree, an evergreen whose scientific name is *Ilex paraguariensis.* Green tea, on the other hand, is native to China and was exported to Japan in about A.D. 800. Its leaves, like the leaves of black tea, come from the *Camellia sinensis* plant.

Another difference between yerba maté and green tea is the way the beverage is brewed. In South America, yerba maté is traditionally brewed in hollow gourds, themselves called matés. The gourd is filled three-quarters full with leaves, which are then covered with boiling water. When that has been completely absorbed, more water is added. The brewed tea is then drunk through a tube with a strainer at one end, called a bombilla. Maté is often served with milk, sugar, or lemon juice to cut its slight bitterness.

Green tea, however, usually is brewed in teapots. Only about a teaspoon of leaves is used per pot. The leaves are steeped for only two minutes or so—much less time than the repeated soaking for yerba maté. Green tea has a mild taste and is served plain in ceramic cups.

No matter how they are brewed and drunk, though, both yerba maté and green tea are thought to offer many health benefits. Each is loaded with antioxidants that may boost the immune system and help prevent cancer. Yerba maté is thought to aid digestion. Similarly, green tea has been reputed to lower cholesterol and blood sugar and relieve the pain of arthritis.

So, no matter which tea you choose—yerba maté or green tea—here's to your health and good taste!

Recognizing Text Structures
Comparison and Contrast 159

SKILL DEVELOPMENT
These activities offer graphic organizers, Mark It Up features, and other reading support to help you comprehend and think critically about the selection.

Test Preparation for All Learners

Lecturas para todos offers models, strategies, and practice to help you prepare for standardized tests.

TEST PREPARATION STRATEGIES

- Successful test taking
- Reading test model and practice—long selections
- Reading test model and practice—short selections
- Functional reading test model and practice
- Revising-and-editing test model and practice
- Writing test model and practice
- Scoring rubrics

Reading Test Model
SHORT SELECTIONS

DIRECTIONS The strategies you have just learned can also help you with this shorter selection, "Tikal." As you read the selection, respond to the notes in the side column.

When you've finished reading, answer the multiple-choice questions. Use the side-column notes to help you understand what each question is asking and why each answer is correct.

Tikal

In the lush tropical rain forest of northern Guatemala lie the ruins of the Maya city of Tikal, the ceremonial center of the ancient Maya civilization. Tikal got its start as a small village during the Middle Formative Period (900–300 B.C.) of Maya civilization. By the Late Formative Period (300 B.C.–A.D. 100), great temples and pyramids signified that the city had become an important ceremonial center.

Ceremony, however, was not the only role Tikal would play in Maya civilization. During the Early Classical Period (A.D. 100–600), Tikal was an important city in a vast trading network that included the central Mexican city of Teotihuacán. By the start of the Late Classical Period (A.D. 600–900), Tikal was a flourishing metropolis with an urban population of 10,000 inhabitants and an outlying population of around 50,000 people. Impressive plazas, palaces, and pyramids filled the city. During this same period,

APUNTES

READING STRATEGIES FOR ASSESSMENT

Note the periods of Maya civilization and their dates. How do these dates help you understand the development of Tikal?

Pay attention to topic sentences. What new information will this paragraph tell you about Tikal?

Revising-and-Editing Test Model

DIRECTIONS Read the following paragraph carefully. Then answer the multiple-choice questions that follow. After answering the questions, read the material in the side columns to check your answer strategies.

[1]Last summer my cousins and me visited Mexico and we spent a morning the city of Taxco. [2] We seen a brochure that said Taxco produced the best silverwork in the Western Hemisphere. [3]Even before the arrival of Columbus, the Native Americans were mining silver and other metals. [4]The Spanish became wealthy from the silver mines. [5]During the colonial period. [6]Because of its history and architecture, Mexico declared Taxco a national monument. [7] We would of stayed longer, but our bus was leaving for the return trip to Mexico City. [8]We plan to go there again one day. [9]We plan to explore the city further.

1. Which of the following is the best way to rewrite the beginning of sentence 1?

   A. Last summer, us cousins...

   B. Last summer, my cousins and I...

   C. Last summer, me and my cousins...

   D. Last summer, I and my cousins...

2. What is the correct way to punctuate the two complete thoughts in sentence 1?

   A. ...visited Mexico: and we...

   B. ...visited Mexico; and we...

   C. ...visited Mexico, and we...

   D. ...visited Mexico—and we...

READING STRATEGIES FOR ASSESSMENT

Watch for common errors. Highlight or underline errors such as incorrect punctuation, spelling, or capitalization; fragments or run-on sentences; and missing or misplaced information.

ANSWER STRATEGIES

Personal Pronouns When deciding whether to use the personal pronoun *me* or *I* in a sentence, think about how the pronoun is used. If it's used as the subject, use *I*. If it's used as an object, use *me*.

Correct Punctuation Sentence 1 is a compound sentence. That is, it has two independent clauses joined by the conjunction *and*. In such cases, the correct punctuation is a comma.

Writing Test Model

DIRECTIONS Many tests ask you to write an essay in response to a writing prompt. A writing prompt is a brief statement that describes a writing situation. Some writing prompts ask you to explain *what, why,* or *how.* Others ask you to convince someone of something.

As you analyze the following writing prompts, read and respond to the notes in the side columns. Then look at the response to each prompt. The notes in the side columns will help you understand why each response is considered strong.

Prompt A

Everyone enjoys leisure time and everyone has a favorite way to enjoy such time. Think about what you like to do most with your leisure time.

Now write an essay that describes your favorite leisure activity. Include details that enable readers to understand and experience your enthusiasm.

Strong Response

Between school and working at my family's hardware store, I don't have much time to myself. However, when I can grab a couple of hours of free time, I love jumping on my bike and riding the back roads just outside of Carpenterville. Whether I'm alone or with friends, a long ride helps clear my mind and refresh my spirit.

I ride a road bike, a lightweight, sleek machine with a red pearl finish. Its drop handlebars, thin tires, and sixteen gears are perfect for propelling me along the gently rolling hills of these parts. I've devised several different routes through the countryside. Some are designed for speed—perfect for those days when I'm looking for a really good workout. Other routes are more scenic. I can take these

APUNTES

ANALYZING THE PROMPT

Identify the topic. Read the first paragraph of the prompt carefully. Underline the topic of the essay you will write.

Understand what's expected of you. The second paragraph of the prompt explains what you must do and offers suggestions on how to create a successful response.

ANSWER STRATEGIES

Grab the reader's attention. This opening paragraph is an invitation to the reader to go riding with the writer and experience what he experiences on his bike.

Provide interesting information. Here the writer describes his bike and the routes he takes, painting a picture for the reader.

Para leer *Un parque tropical de Costa Rica*

Reading Strategy

CHART YOUR PREFERENCES Keep track of what interests you in this chart. In the first column, list the park attractions. In the second, rate each one, from 1 (not interesting) to 3 (very interesting). In the third column, write the reason for your rating.

Atracciones de Buru Ri Ri	Me gusta (1–3)	¿Por qué?

What You Need to Know

Costa Rica is well known for its ecotourism. This small country is famous for its abundant wildlife as well as the exotic and threatened ecosystems it is trying to preserve. Costa Rica's national parks cover almost 12% of the land; biological reserves and wildlife refuges are abundant too. Visitors hope to see some of the more than 850 species of birds and 600 species of exotic mammals—including three-toed sloth, tapirs, coatis, giant anteaters, peccaries, and jungle cats. Tropical flowers such as orchids and bromeliads also abound. Parks like the one described here attract tourists from around the world.

Un parque tropical de Costa Rica

Bienvenidos a Buru Ri Ri

Un día de aventura[1] en la **naturaleza costarricense**

Actividades

Teleférico Viaja en cabinas que cuelgan[2] de un cable a una altura[3] de 265 pies. Seis personas viajan en cada cabina donde tienen vistas **panorámicas** del parque.

Jardín de mariposas[4] Visita nuestra estructura dedicada a cientos de mariposas. Aprende del ciclo de vida[5] de estos insectos.

Jardines tropicales Conoce la naturaleza de Costa Rica. En los jardines encuentras zonas dedicadas a diferentes plantas como orquídeas[6], bromelias[7] y los árboles de nuestros **bosques lluviosos.** También puedes ver los pájaros[8] coloridos de los bosques.

Aventuras Actividades para el aventurero incluyen **montar a caballo** o deslizarse[9] en el Cable Fantástico, un cable donde viajas en el aire a una velocidad de casi 80 kilómetros por hora. También puedes viajar por encima del parque en nuestro sistema de plataformas y cables. Es el sistema más grande del país.

Restaurantes Tenemos dos restaurantes que sirven auténtica comida costarricense.

---

[1] adventure   [2] hang   [3] height   [4] butterflies
[5] **ciclo...** life cycle   [6] orchids   [7] bromeliads   [8] birds
[9] slide

PALABRAS CLAVE

la naturaleza *nature*
costarricense *Costa Rican*
viajar *to travel*

panorámica *scenic*
el bosque lluvioso *rain forest*
montar a caballo *horseback riding*

READING TIP This brochure about Buru Ri Ri breaks the information down into short sections. Before you read, look at the headings to anticipate the kinds of facts you will find out about the park. You can also use the headings to help you find specific pieces of information.

MÁRCALO GRAMÁTICA You have already studied and reviewed regular **-ar** verbs. Though the endings of these verbs change for each person, the stems always remain the same. Look over this page of the brochure and circle at least three regular **-ar** verbs.

APUNTES

READER'S SUCCESS STRATEGY This reading contains many **cognates,** words that are similar to English words that have the same meaning. Before looking up an unfamiliar word, first decide whether it looks like an English word you know and determine whether the meaning of the English word makes sense in the context of the reading.

A pensar...

1. What sort of person would enjoy a trip to Buru Ri Ri? **(Infer)**

_____

_____

_____

2. Which tour would you take if you were the very adventurous type? **(Infer)**

_____

_____

_____

CHALLENGE

1. What is the purpose of this brochure? Why would someone write for this purpose? **(Understanding Author's Purpose)**

_____

_____

_____

_____

2. Has the writer of the brochure succeeded in his or her purpose? How do you know? **(Make Judgments)**

_____

_____

_____

_____

Buru Ri Ri

¿Dónde queda el parque Buru Ri Ri?

Queda en el valle central de Costa Rica. Está cerca de la capital, San José, y cerca también de la costa Pacífica.

¿Cuánto cuesta una visita?

Precios de entrada*	Adultos	Estudiantes**	Niños†
Tour básico del parque Buru Ri Ri	$45	$40	$35
Tour de aventura (Selecciona uno: Montar a caballo, Cable fantástico o Tour de plataformas)	$45	$40	$35
Tour extremo (Dos horas en las plataformas más otra actividad de aventura)	$60	$55	$50

* Los precios del tour incluyen: viaje en autobús de San José, comida, un viaje en Teleférico y un(a) guía bilingüe.

**Precio de estudiante: es necesario presentar la identificación de estudiante.

† (de 3 a 11 años)

Sugerencias para tu visita

Habla con tu agente de viajes para incluir una visita al Parque Tropical BURU RI RI en tu **itinerario.**

Para más información:

Parque Tropical BURU RI RI
Apdo. 571-2100
Tel: (591) – 280-1234
www. bururiri.com

PALABRAS CLAVE
itinerario _itinerary_

Vocabulario de la lectura

Palabras clave

el bosque lluvioso *rain forest*   **la naturaleza** *nature*
costarricense *Costa Rican*   **panorámica** *scenic*
itinerario *itinerary*   **viajar** *to travel*
montar a caballo *horseback riding*

A. Look at the word pairs. On the lines next to each pair, write whether these words are synonyms or antonyms.

1. naturaleza – medio ambiente   _____

2. bosques lluviosos – junglas   _____

3. viajar – quedarse   _____

4. itinerario – horario   _____

5. montar a caballo – caminar   _____

B. Complete the sentences using words from the **Palabras clave.**

1. Marcos es de Costa Rica. Es _____.

2. Muchos animales raros viven en los _____ de Costa Rica.

3. Mira el _____ para saber adónde vamos mañana.

4. Aquí tenemos una vista _____ de toda la ciudad.

5. A Marisol no le gusta _____ lejos de su casa.

¿Comprendiste?

1. ¿Cuáles son las actividades que puedes hacer en el Parque Buru Ri Ri?

_____

_____

_____

2. ¿Dónde queda el parque?

_____

_____

3. ¿Por qué cuesta más el tour extremo?

_____

Conexión personal

Write about one special experience you had when visiting a natural area. Write short answers to the questions below in the organizer. Then bring your ideas together in a few sentences about your experience.

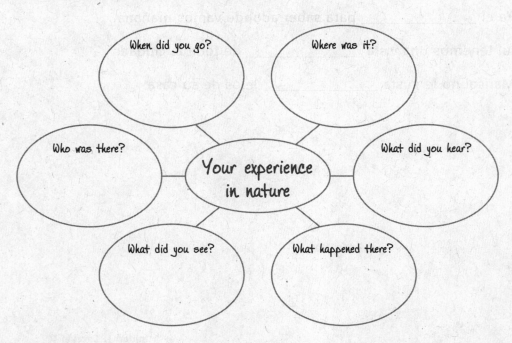

Para leer   *De vacaciones: Costa Rica y Chile*

Reading Strategy

USE A VENN DIAGRAM TO COMPARE Compare Costa Rica and
Chile using this Venn diagram. List *similarities* in the overlapping
space. List *differences* in the two outside circles.

Costa Rica   Chile

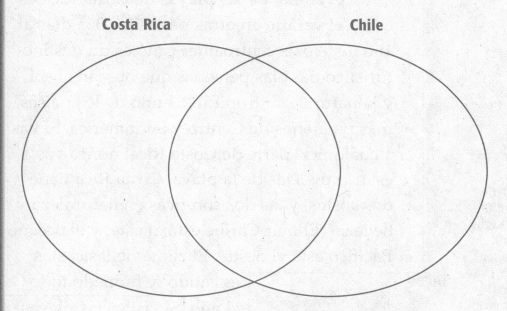

What You Need to Know

Interested in travel for all seasons? Costa Rica and Chile offer vacation
choices for sun worshipers and snow birds. Those who love the ocean can
enjoy year-round swimming weather at Costa Rica's beaches. In addition
to swimming and scuba diving, visitors can enjoy fishing for large game
fish such as marlin and tarpon. Costa Rica is also a surfer's paradise, with
resorts on both coasts offering special packages for surfers. In contrast, the
Andean peaks of Chile offer some of the best skiing in the world during
the Southern Hemisphere's winter. Skiers flock to resorts such as Portillo
and Termas de Chillán for their sensational skiing and snowboarding,
unparalleled scenery, and comfortable accommodations. Portillo is just over
the ridge from Aconcagua, the highest peak in the western hemisphere.

Take notes as you read to compare and contrast both countries. Make a chart with two columns, one for each country. Note items such as geography, climate, and sports activities.

Costa Rica	Chile

▥ MÁRCALO > GRAMÁTICA

You have already studied the distinction between the verbs **ser** and **estar**, which both mean "to be." Look through the boxed text and circle two instances in which the verb **ser** is used and two instances in which **estar** is used. Think about why the verb is used in each instance.

★ READER'S SUCCESS STRATEGY When you feel Costa Rica's warmth along its beaches or you imagine the long tall mountains of Chile, you are visualizing. Pay attention to all the images that form in your mind as you read about these two places.

De vacaciones: Costa Rica y Chile 🎧

¿**C**ómo te gustaría pasar tus vacaciones? ¿Prefieres nadar en el **mar**, esquiar o hacer snowboard? Costa Rica y Chile ofrecen posibilidades para cada preferencia.

5   El clima[1] de las **playas** de Costa Rica es como el **verano** en otras partes los 365 días al año. Este país centroamericano es un destino turístico para las personas que buscan el sol y la naturaleza[2] tropical. Es uno de los países
10 más pequeños de Centro y Sudamérica. Si vas a cualquier[3] parte de Costa Rica, nunca vas a estar muy lejos de la playa. Costa Rica tiene dos costas, y las dos son ricas en naturaleza y belleza[4]. El mar Caribe está al este[5] y el océano
15 Pacífico está al oeste[6]. El clima de las costas es cálido[7] y húmedo todo el año. Si visitas las playas de Costa Rica puedes pasar tus vacaciones haciendo
20 actividades tan diversas como nadar o **bucear** en el agua cristalina, explorar

La playa Jacó, en la costa del Océano Pacífico, Costa Rica

---

[1] climate; weather   [2] nature   [3] any   [4] beauty
[5] east   [6] west   [7] warm

PALABRAS CLAVE
el mar *ocean*   **el verano** *summer*
la playa *beach*   **bucear** *to snorkel*

Una atracción de Pucón es hacer snowboard por uno de los volcanes más activos de Chile.

los **arrecifes**, dar caminatas o montar a caballo por la playa

25 o por los bosques[8] tropicales que llegan hasta el lado del mar.

Chile es un país de extremos, largo y **estrecho**, pero

30 de área pequeña. Queda entre[9] las montañas de los Andes y el océano Pacífico. Es un lugar de variación climática donde hay veranos **cálidos** y secos[10] e inviernos fríos con lluvia y nieve. Cuando

35 el clima cambia al **invierno**—entre los meses de junio a septiembre— hay lugares en Chile a lo largo[11] de la **cordillera** de los Andes que se convierten en destinos turísticos para las personas en busca de la **nieve** y la

40 aventura. Aquí los aficionados de los deportes del invierno llegan desde todas partes del hemisferio norte. Llegan para esquiar o hacer snowboard y para disfrutar[12] del invierno chileno.

---

[8] forests   [9] between   [10] dry
[11] **a lo...** along   [12] enjoy

A pensar...

If you love winter sports, when would you want to vacation in Chile? Why? **(Draw Conclusions)**

_____

_____

_____

_____

CHALLENGE According to the reading, how is the geography of Costa Rica different from the geography in Chile? **(Compare and Contrast)**

_____

_____

_____

_____

_____

_____

_____

_____

PALABRAS CLAVE

el arrecife *coral reef*
estrecho(a) *narrow*
cálido(a) *warm*

el invierno *winter*
la cordillera *mountain range*
la nieve *snow*

Vocabulario de la lectura

Palabras clave

el arrecife	*coral reef*	**el invierno**	*winter*
bucear	*to snorkel*	**el mar**	*ocean*
cálido	*warm*	**la nieve**	*snow*
la cordillera	*mountain range*	**la playa**	*beach*
estrecho(a)	*narrow*	**el verano**	*summer*

A. Using **Palabras clave,** complete the sentences below.

1. El clima de Costa Rica siempre es _____.

2. En Costa Rica; nunca estás lejos de la _____.

3. Si quieres ver animales marinos interesantes, puedes _____ y

explorar los _____.

4. Costa Rica tiene costas en el _____ Caribe.

5. Hay montañas muy altas en la _____ de los Andes.

B. Write the letter for the word or phrase that goes best with each **Palabra clave.**

_____ **1.** invierno   a. típica del invierno

_____ **2.** estrecho   b. enero

_____ **3.** nieve   c. julio

_____ **4.** verano   d. con poco espacio

¿Comprendiste?

1. Describe el clima de Costa Rica y el clima de Chile. ¿Cuáles son las diferencias?

_____

_____

2. ¿Puedes encontrar los dos países en un mapa? ¿Puedes explicar por qué los climas son diferentes?

_____

_____

3. ¿En qué país te gustaría pasar las vacaciones? ¿Por qué?

_____

_____

Conexión personal

You are writing a journal entry about a favorite vacation experience, whether in the winter or summer. What made it so much fun?

Mis vacaciones favoritas

Para leer   *La Copa Mundial*

Reading Strategy

MAKE A GRAPH To understand the reading better, graph the number of wins by each country mentioned as a *ganador*. Complete the graph below.

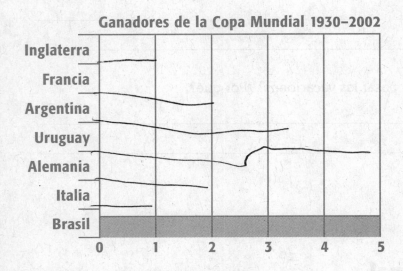

Ganadores de la Copa Mundial 1930–2002

What You Need to Know

One of the most eagerly anticipated international sporting events in the world is the World Cup of soccer, which takes place every four years. The best national teams worldwide compete for this title. FIFA *(Fédération Internationale de Football Association)*, which organizes the tournament, was founded in Paris in 1904. It celebrated its hundredth anniversary in 2004 with a centennial match between Brazil and France. The World Cup was the brainchild of FIFA president Jules Rimet. Twenty-four national teams entered the first tournament in 1930. In 2006, 32 competing nations played against each other in Germany. FIFA itself has grown to include more than 200 member associations, thus making it one of the largest and certainly the most popular sports federations in the world.

La Copa Mundial 🎧

No hay otro evento deportivo que pueda **captar** la atención del **mundo** como lo hace la Copa Mundial de la FIFA (Fédération Internationale de Football Association). Lee estas tarjetas para saber la historia de esta competencia internacional.

El trofeo original del torneo se llama La Copa Jules Rimet. Brasil adquirió este trofeo después de ganar su tercera Copa Mundial en 1970. El nuevo trofeo está en uso desde 1974 y el país que lo gana, lo conserva por cuatro años hasta la siguiente competencia.

Desde su primera edición, celebrada en Uruguay en 1930, la Copa Mundial de la FIFA ha crecido[1] en popularidad. En esta competencia los mejores **equipos** de fútbol de todos los países compiten por el título de campeón del mundo. La idea se originó[2] gracias a un grupo de visionarios franceses en 1920. Su líder fue el innovador Jules Rimet. Después de diez años la idea se hizo[3] realidad y el primer campeonato fue en 1930. Desde ese año, ha habido[4] 16 torneos, en los cuales ganaron sólo siete campeones **distintos.** La **única** interrupción en el torneo fue por la Segunda Guerra Mundial[5]

Hoy en día la Copa Mundial capta la atención de todos los aficionados a fútbol del planeta. Hay una audiencia global de más de 3.700 millones de personas. Y la **meta** de los **jugadores** y los aficionados sigue siendo lo mismo: ganar el trofeo, la Copa.

LA COPA MUNDIAL

---

[1] **ha...** has grown
[2] **se...** originated
[3] **se...** became
[4] **ha...** there have been
[5] **Segunda...** World War II

PALABRAS CLAVE

captar *to capture*	**distinto(a)** *different*
el mundo *world*	**único(a)** *only*
adquirir *to acquire*	**la meta** *goal*
el equipo *team*	**el jugador** *player*

READING TIP In most of the Spanish-speaking world, periods and commas within numbers are the reverse of the way they appear in U.S. English. For example in Spain the number 3,500.8 would be written 3.500,8. In Mexico, Central America, and Puerto Rico, numbers are usually punctuated as they are in the United States.

║║║MÁRCALO ⟩ GRAMÁTICA
Demonstrative adjectives and pronouns are used to emphasize a noun or to distinguish one thing from another. Circle two demonstrative adjectives and the nouns they emphasize in the boxed text.

Tables help you find facts quickly and easily. The table in this reading tells you the World Cup winners for each year the tournament was played. Even a quick glance at the table will tell you which teams have dominated the World Cup, which teams have occasionally made it to second place, and what types of scores are typical for championship soccer games.

A pensar...

Look at the table of first- and second-place teams. Which two continents are represented? What does this tell you about soccer on these continents? **(Draw Conclusions)**

_____

_____

_____

_____

CHALLENGE Is soccer popular in your community? Do you believe professional soccer will become more popular in the United States? Why? Use your own knowledge about soccer in your community and country to answer the questions. **(Connect, Activate Prior Knowledge, Predict)**

_____

_____

_____

_____

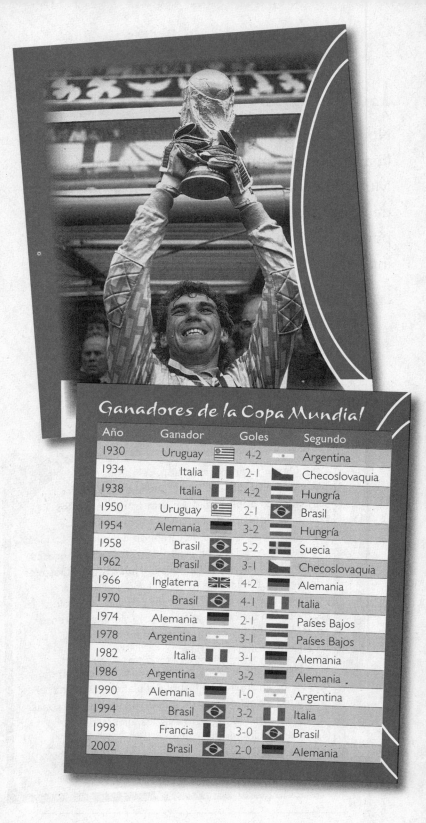

Ganadores de la Copa Mundial

Año	Ganador	Goles	Segundo
1930	Uruguay	4-2	Argentina
1934	Italia	2-1	Checoslovaquia
1938	Italia	4-2	Hungría
1950	Uruguay	2-1	Brasil
1954	Alemania	3-2	Hungría
1958	Brasil	5-2	Suecia
1962	Brasil	3-1	Checoslovaquia
1966	Inglaterra	4-2	Alemania
1970	Brasil	4-1	Italia
1974	Alemania	2-1	Países Bajos
1978	Argentina	3-1	Países Bajos
1982	Italia	3-1	Alemania
1986	Argentina	3-2	Alemania
1990	Alemania	1-0	Argentina
1994	Brasil	3-2	Italia
1998	Francia	3-0	Brasil
2002	Brasil	2-0	Alemania

Vocabulario de la lectura

Palabras clave

adquirir *to acquire*	**el jugador** *player*
captar *to capture*	**la meta** *goal*
distinto(a) *different*	**el mundo** *world*
el equipo *team*	**único(a)** *only*

A. Write the letter of the synonym for each of the **Palabras clave.**

_D_ **1.** mundo   a. capturar

_A_ **2.** captar   b. ganar

_e_ **3.** meta   c. diferente

_b_ **4.** distinto   d. planeta

_C_ **5.** adquirir   e. objetivo

B. Fill in the blanks with the correct form of a **Palabra clave.**

1. Los ___equipos___ querían ganar el trofeo para su país.

2. El ___único___ de Brasil ganó la Copa Mundial cinco veces.

3. La ___jugador___ vez que Francia ganó la Copa Mundial fue en 1998.

4. Posiblemente la Copa Mundial es el torneo deportivo más popular

del ___adquirir___ .

5. Todos los países quieren ___mundo___ el trofeo de oro.

¿Comprendiste?

1. ¿En qué año empezó la Copa Mundial?

2002

2. ¿Cómo se llama el trofeo? ¿Por qué tiene ese nombre?

la Copa mundial porque todos competran

3. ¿Con qué frecuencia ocurre la Copa Mundial?

los equipos

4. ¿Quién ganó la Copa Mundial más que todos los otros países?

Brasl

5. ¿Por qué no jugaron una Copa Mundial entre 1938 y 1950?

porque avra problemas.

Conexión personal

Write a paragraph about your favorite sports team. What is their record like? Have they ever won the championship or made it to the championship tournament? Why are they your favorite team?

Mi equipo preferido es...

no tengo un
equipo porque
no me
gusta sports

Para leer   *Vivir de la tierra*

Reading Strategy

USE WORD FAMILIES Guess the meaning of at least five new words based on "word families." For example, *cafetero* is in the same word family as *café.* Complete the table showing the familiar word, the new word, and its meaning.

Palabra que ya sé	Palabra nueva	Definición
café	cafetero	Cafeterra
~~Augus~~ tomo	~~Au~~ toma	tomar
Quien	Quero	quienes
Acer	Acero	Aceros
cundido	cundos	cuande ?

What You Need to Know

Much of central Argentina is covered by the Pampas, a vast, flat, plain. This fertile land produces many of the country's agricultural crops and is home to Argentina's legendary cowboys, the *gauchos*. The number of *gauchos* has diminished in recent years as young people move to the cities, but many cattlemen are proud to preserve this lifestyle.

In the mountains of Colombia, coffee growing is a key industry. Coffee was first discovered in Eastern Africa. In time, its use spread to Turkey. In the 1700s, a French captain brought a coffee plant to the Caribbean island of Martinique. Coffee eventually made its way to the rest of tropical South and Central America.

Vivir de la tierra

La vida[1] del gaucho es la vida de un **ganadero** que vive de **la**
5 **tierra**. La región del gaucho es La Pampa, tierra

Un gaucho argentino en ropa tradicional

de mucho sol y de **llanos**. Estas condiciones determinan lo que hace el gaucho día a día.
10 Los gauchos se levantan **temprano** para atender el ganado[2] y para mantener los ranchos. El «**sueldo**» del gaucho es la carne y la piel del ganado que vende.

Estas condiciones también definen qué
15 ropa se pone y qué comida comen él y su familia regularmente. Para trabajar, se pone un sombrero grande para protegerse del sol, del viento y de la **lluvia**. Se pone pantalones que se llaman «bombachas» y unas botas
20 altas. En la casa del gaucho comen lo que

[1] life   [2] cattle

Las pampas de Argentina, la tierra del gaucho

PALABRAS CLAVE

el ganadero *cattle rancher*	**temprano** *early*
la tierra *land, soil*	**el sueldo** *salary*
el llano *prairie*	**la lluvia** *rain*

produce el gaucho: por ejemplo, el asado—
una variedad de carnes— es el plato típico de
los gauchos.

Las montañas[3] de Colombia son ideales
25 para el cultivo del café: son húmedas, altas
y **frescas.** En Colombia, el café es muy
importante. Hay una «cultura del café». El
café colombiano es famoso también en otros
países: es uno de los mejores del mundo[4].

30 El cafetero colombiano debe trabajar la
tierra constantemente. ¿Cómo es un día típico
de un cafetero? Los cafeteros se acuestan
temprano y se levantan muy temprano todos
los días. Normalmente se despiertan entre
35 las dos y las cuatro de la mañana. Se arreglan
para salir: se ponen la ruana, o poncho, y
el sombrero grande. Algunos todavía van
en mula[5] a su trabajo, una tradición de los
cafeteros. Van a los campos todos los días para
40 cultivar y mantener[6] el café. Más tarde, deben
sacar los granos de café[7] porque luego tienen
que prepararlos para convertirlos en la famosa
bebida.

---

[3] mountains   [4] world   [5] mule
[6] maintain   [7] **granos**… coffee beans

Un cafetero colombiano saca los granos de café.

Cultivos de café, cerca de Armenia, Colombia

PALABRAS CLAVE
fresco(a)   *cool*

Why do you think some cafeteros still ride mules to their work? **(Draw Conclusions)**

_____

_____

_____

_____

_____

_____

☐ MÁRCALO ⟩ GRAMÁTICA
You have just learned about reflexive verbs, verbs that take a form of the pronoun **se.** In the boxed text, circle at least three reflexive verbs.

_____

_____

_____

_____

_____

_____

_____

_____

_____

Vocabulario de la lectura

Palabras clave

    fresco(a)   *cool*

    el ganadero   *cattle rancher*

    el llano   *prairie*

    la lluvia   *rain*

    el sueldo   *salary*

    temprano   *early*

    la tierra   *land, soil*

A. Complete each sentence by writing one of the **Palabras clave** in the blank.

  1. La Pampa es la _____ de los gauchos.

  2. Los _____ de las Pampas son todos iguales, sin altos ni bajos.

  3. Los gauchos y los cafeteros se despiertan _____.

  4. Cuando hace _____ me pongo un suéter.

  5. Con el sombrero se protege del agua de la _____.

B. Find the synonym for each **Palabra clave.** Write the letter for the synonym in the blank.

  _____ **1.** el ganadero   a. precipitación

  _____ **2.** el sueldo   b. ranchero

  _____ **3.** la lluvia   c. un poco frío

  _____ **4.** fresco(a)   d. salario

¿Comprendiste?

1. ¿Cómo se llama la región de Argentina donde viven los gauchos?

_____

2. ¿Cuáles son las actividades del gaucho? ¿Qué produce el gaucho? ¿El cafetero?

_____

_____

3. ¿Qué se pone un gaucho para trabajar? ¿Un cafetero?

_____

_____

4. Compara la rutina diaria del gaucho con la rutina del cafetero. ¿A qué hora se levantan? ¿Qué se ponen?

_____

_____

_____

Conexión personal

Look at the daily routine of the *gaucho* and the coffee grower, and write their activities in the chart below. Then write your own daily activities. How might your day be more interesting than that of a *gaucho* or *cafetero,* or why might it be more boring? Use details from the chart to explain your reasons.

LA RUTINA DIARIA

El gaucho	El cafetero	Yo

Para leer   *Revista de moda*

Reading Strategy

DRAW TWO PICTURES OF YOUR CLOSET Draw a picture below of
your own closet that shows where you now put different types of
clothes, shoes, and other items. Then draw a picture that shows
how you could reorganize it by following the directions in the
reading.

What You Need to Know

Are you tired of searching for the clothes you want every morning? Do your
best shoes get lost or even damaged in your closet? There's a solution! A
thoughtfully organized closet can make your life easier and take some of
the hassle out of getting ready in the morning. In articles like this one, you'll
find many useful tips for keeping your belongings organized.

Revista de moda

¿Estás cansado de buscar tu ropa en un clóset desorganizado? Este artículo presenta ideas que te van a ayudar.

¡Organiza tu clóset!

Tener un clóset organizado te lo hace todo más fácil.

Primero, saca todo lo que tienes del clóset. Separa la ropa que usas mucho de la ropa que casi no usas.

De la ropa que no usas frecuentemente, escoge lo que ya no está de moda o lo que ya no te queda. Pon toda esta ropa en una bolsa[1] de plástico y dásela a una **organización filantrópica.**

1 La ropa formal, como vestidos o trajes: Debes **guardarla** en plástico a un lado del clóset. Debes **colgar** al otro lado la ropa que más usas.

2 Camisas, blusas, chalecos: Organízalos por colores y tipo de ropa.

3 Jeans y pantalones: Puedes **doblar** y colgarlos en ganchos de varios Leveles[2] para tener más espacio. Muchachas, es buena idea hacer esto con las faldas también.

*Si tienes **estantes** en el clóset, debes poner allí la ropa que puedes doblar.*

---

[1] bag   [2] levels

PALABRAS CLAVE
la organización filantrópica *charity*
guardar *to put away; to keep*
colgar *to hang*
doblar *to fold*
el estante *shelf*

READING TIP The command form of a verb is normally used for giving suggestions or instructions. For example, **saca, lee, aprende,** and **separa** are commands. Although these verbs seem to have no subject, the subject *you* is understood.

CHALLENGE Pay attention to the images that form in your mind as you read these suggestions from a fashion expert, and try to picture your own closet organized according to the ideas in the article. **(Visualize)**

Then look at the closets in this magazine article again, and write a paragraph that compares and contrasts both closets. **(Compare and Contrast)**

_____

_____

_____

_____

_____

READER'S SUCCESS STRATEGY Underline the different ideas the author in this article gives on how to organize your closet. Then look at them to see if they make sense. Usually, you can grasp details more clearly if you underline the main points.

1. What is this article about? **(Identifying Main Idea)**

_____

_____

_____

_____

_____

_____

2. Who might read an article like this? **(Infer)**

_____

_____

_____

_____

_____

_____

_____

_____

_____

_____

_____

_____

Para los que viven lejos de su país tropical, también deben tener ropa para el frío.

- Durante el invierno, guarda toda tu ropa de verano en una maleta o caja[3].
- Durante el verano, guarda la ropa de invierno en la maleta donde guardaste la ropa de verano.

 4 Camisetas: Organízalas por colores y tipos.

 5 Ropa deportiva: Pon toda tu ropa de ejercicio en un lugar.

 6 Suéteres: Ponlos todos juntos y organízalos por colores y tipos.

 7 Abrigos: Puedes colgar los que usas frecuentemente en un gancho en la puerta. Puedes colgar los otros al **fondo** del clóset.

[3] box

PALABRAS CLAVE
el fondo _back, bottom_

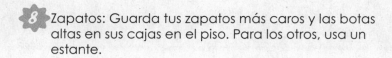

8 Zapatos: Guarda tus zapatos más caros y las botas altas en sus cajas en el piso. Para los otros, usa un estante.

9 Usa un **gancho** largo en la puerta para colgar tus correas y otras cosas.

10 En la parte de arriba, puedes guardar: (muchachos) tu mochila, tus gorras y cosas extras; (muchachas) tu mochila, tus carteras[4] y otros accesorios.

CHALLENGE Go over the author's ideas for better closet organization. Then write the various steps in an ordered list. **(Paraphrase, Chronological Order)**

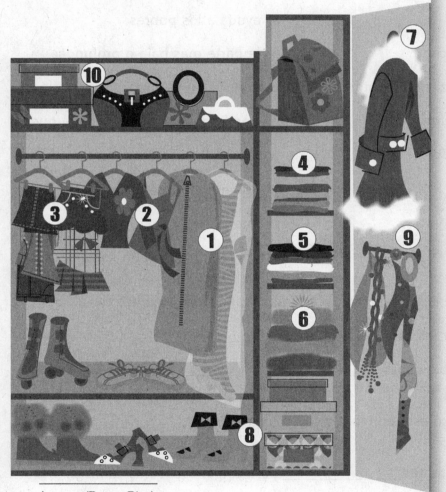

[4] purses (Puerto Rico)

PALABRAS CLAVE
el gancho   *hook*   guardar   *to put away, keep*

Vocabulario de la lectura

Palabras clave

colgar *to hang*
doblar *to fold*
el estante *shelf*
el fondo *back, bottom*

el gancho *hook*
guardar *to put away; to keep*
la organización filantrópica *charity*

A. Match the words with the definitions.

_____ **1.** colgar

_____ **2.** el gancho

_____ **3.** organización filantrópica

_____ **4.** el estante

_____ **5.** el fondo

_____ **6.** doblar

_____ **7.** guardar

a. ayuda a los pobres

b. la parte más baja o profunda

c. meter algo en una caja o un clóset

d. donde puedes poner la ropa que no cuelgas

e. lo que haces con la ropa antes de ponerla en un estante

f. objeto para colgar la ropa

g. poner la ropa en un gancho

B. Complete each sentence with the correct form of one of the **Palabras clave.**

1. Puedes poner los zapatos y las carteras en _____.

2. My amiga trabaja para _____ que da ropa a las personas que no tienen mucho dinero.

3. Casi nunca uso este abrigo. Lo voy a colgar en _____ de mi clóset.

4. No tengo bastantes _____ para colgar todas mis camisas.

5. Luz María _____ todos sus suéteres en una maleta.

¿Comprendiste?

1. ¿Qué debes hacer primero para organizar tu clóset?

_____

2. ¿Cómo debes organizar las camisetas y los suéteres?

_____

3. ¿Qué recomienda el artículo para la ropa de verano y de invierno?

_____

_____

4. ¿Cuáles son las diferencias entre el clóset del chico y el clóset de la chica?

_____

Conexión personal

What could you do to make your closet more organized and user-friendly? What clothes would you keep and what would you give away? Picture your closet as it is now and write three things you would like to do to improve it.

Mi clóset

Cosas que quiero	Cosas que no quiero
_____	_____
_____	_____
_____	_____
_____	_____

Ideas que tengo para mejorar mi clóset

_____

_____

_____

Para leer   *Las artesanías*

Reading Strategy

DRAW A MIND MAP OF COUNTRIES AND CRAFTS Add onto this
mind map to show the key facts about crafts in Panama and Puerto
Rico. Include as many circles and details as possible.

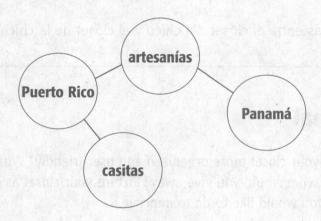

What You Need to Know

The arts and cultures of Latin America arise from a mixture of influences.
The Taíno people lived on the island of Puerto Rico before the Spanish
explorers arrived, and while the Taínos have disappeared, elements of their
culture live on. The *tallas de santos* are inspired by the Catholic religion
that arrived with the Spaniards. Among the most popular figures are *los tres
reyes,* the Three Kings. In Panama, indigenous peoples such as the Cuna
still live in some areas. Rich artistic traditions, such as the making of *molas,*
have helped indigenous groups survive, as the beautiful handicrafts are
popular with tourists and collectors worldwide.

Las artesanías

Tallas de madera:
Los tres reyes

Hay muchas artesanías típicas de Puerto Rico. Dos muy **conocidas** son la **talla** de santos[1] y las «casitas». Las tallas son figuras de madera que representan a los santos de la tradición

5

social puertorriqueña. Primero, el artesano o la artesana trabaja la madera; luego la pinta.

10 Estas tallas llevan símbolos que identifican al santo. Las casitas son fachadas[2] en miniatura de casas y **edificios** históricos. Existen de muchos **tamaños** y materiales: las más famosas son de cerámica y son muy finas. Hay

15 también algunas de madera y otras que son básicamente pinturas sobre madera o metal. Las fachadas pueden ser de casas históricas, pero también pueden ser de edificios importantes o de lugares tradicionales,

---

[1] saints   [2] façades

Una casita de cerámica (a la izquierda); la calle Tetuán,
Viejo San Juan (a la derecha)

PALABRAS CLAVE

conocido(a) *well known*	**el edificio** *building*
la talla *carving*	**el tamaño** *size*

READING TIP Artesanía is a word that does not have a precise, one-word translation in English. It is generally translated as "handicraft" or "objects made by hand." **Artesanías** reflect the culture of the people who made them and are generally part of a folk art tradition.

READER'S SUCCESS STRATEGY Look at the photos and read the captions before you begin the reading. These visuals will help you understand the written descriptions of some Puerto Rican and Panamanian folk art expressions. After you have finished the reading, look at the photos again to appreciate the beauty of these objects now that you know more about them.

You have learned the present tense of many irregular verbs. In the boxed text, circle the three different irregular verbs.

A pensar...

Which **artesanía** pictured here appeals to you the most? Why? **(Connect)**

_____

_____

_____

_____

CHALLENGE Suppose that you have made miniature drawings for many years. What might cause your work to be thought of as **artesanías? (Evaluate)**

_____

_____

_____

_____

_____

_____

_____

_____

_____

_____

_____

20 como la de Puig y Abraham, en el Viejo San Juan, que hoy en día es un restaurante muy popular.

En Panamá también hay ricas tradiciones de artesanías. Las molas son una 25 de éstas. Las molas son **telas** de colores **vivos, cortadas** y **cosidas** en diseños[3] del mundo[4] de los cunas. Los cunas, una comunidad indígena[5] de Panamá, hacen estas telas que se conocen internacionalmente. En partes de 30 Panamá también hay artesanos que trabajan la cerámica. Por ejemplo, en el pueblo[6] de La Arena, los artesanos hacen trabajo de cerámica con la **arena** del lugar. Ellos decoran sus piezas con diseños de la tradición indígena. 35 Las cerámicas de La Arena son únicas.

---

[3] designs   [4] world   [5] native   [6] town

Una mola tradicional decorada con un pájaro de muchos colores

PALABRAS CLAVE

la tela _fabric_	**cosido(a)** _sewn_
vivo(a) _bright, lively_	**la arena** _sand_
cortado(a) _cut_	

Vocabulario de la lectura

Palabras clave

la arena *sand*
conocido(a) *well known*
cortado(a) *cut*
cosido(a) *sewn*
el edificio *building*

la talla *carving*
el tamaño *size*
la tela *fabric*
vivo(a) *bright, lively*

A. Find the word or expression that goes with each word in the first column. Write the letter of the word or expression in the blank.

_____ **1.** conocida

_____ **2.** el edificio

_____ **3.** vivo

_____ **4.** cortado

_____ **5.** la talla

a. ...con las tijeras

b. brillante (color)

c. una celebridad

d. una casa

e. escultura de madera

B. Complete each sentence with one of the Palabras clave.

1. Las _____ son de madera.

2. En este pueblo famoso de Estados Unidos se pueden encontrar

casitas típicas de San Antonio en todos _____.

3. Los artesanos usan _____ que encuentran en la playa.

4. _____ tradicionales como las molas también se encuentran en otros países, con otros nombres.

5. En muchos países, las telas son _____ para crear artesanías y ropa tradicional.

¿Comprendiste?

1. ¿Qué son las tallas puertorriqueñas?

_____

2. ¿De qué materiales se hacen las «casitas» o fachadas en miniatura?

_____

_____

3. ¿Qué son las molas? ¿Quiénes las hacen?

_____

_____

4. ¿De dónde vienen las ideas y los diseños de los artesanos puertorriqueños y los panameños? ¿Por qué son diferentes las artesanías únicas de estos dos países?

_____

_____

Conexión personal

A museum has asked you to propose a favorite *artesanía* for their upcoming exhibition. Think of a folk art piece you have in your home or that you have seen. It could be from your region or any place in the world. Write a short text for the piece to appear next to it during the exhibit, including the type of *artesanía,* materials it is made of, and a one-sentence description.

Artesanía
_____

_____

Materiales
_____

_____

Descripción
_____

_____

Para leer *Una leyenda mazateca*

Reading Strategy

USE ARROWS TO TRACK THE STORYLINE To track the storyline, write each event on a separate arrow, showing how one event leads to the next. If you need more arrows, you can draw the chart on a separate sheet of paper.

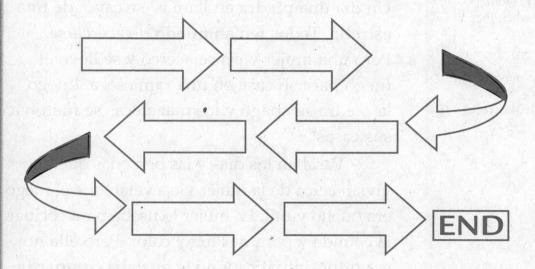

What You Need to Know

Myths, legends, and folktales are traditional stories based on universal truths. They explain the creation of the world, the origins of mankind, and the relationship of humanity to the mysteries of the universe. These stories can help us understand the world views of the cultures in which they originated. Joseph Campbell, a leading authority on myth, explains that these stories all follow similar patterns. This Mazateca legend has similarities to the Native American lore of Coyote stealing fire, the Australian aboriginal folktale of Robin, who robbed flames from a cockatoo, and even the Greek myth of Prometheus.

Una leyenda mazateca: El fuego y el tlacuache

Hay muchas versiones de la leyenda sobre los orígenes del fuego. Ésta es la que cuentan los mazatecas que viven en la región norte de Oaxaca.

Hace muchos **siglos,** en el principio de los tiempos, las personas no conocían el **fuego.** Un día una **piedra** en llamas[1] se cayó[2] de una **estrella**. Todos tenían **miedo** de acercarse[3].

5　Pero una mujer vieja se acercó y se llevó el fuego para su casa en una **rama** seca. Luego la piedra se apagó y los mazatecas se fueron a sus casas.

　　Pasaban los días y las personas que
10　vivían cerca de la mujer vieja veían que el fuego era bueno y útil. La mujer lo usaba para cocinar la comida y para dar luz y calor. Pero ella no era muy simpática y no le gustaba **compartir**. Cuando los mazatecas le pedían un poco de

15　fuego, siempre les decía que no.

[1] flames　　　[2] **se...** fell
[3] to approach

PALABRAS CLAVE
el siglo *century*	**el miedo** *fear*
el fuego *fire*	**la rama** *branch*
la piedra *stone, rock*	**compartir** *to share*
la estrella *star*	

Un día llegó un tlacuache[4] inteligente y les dijo a los mazatecas que él podía traerles
20 el fuego. Los mazatecas pensaban que eso era imposible. Si ellos no lo podían hacer, ¿cómo lo iba a hacer ese pequeño animal? Pero el tlacuache insistió en que él lo podía hacer y que les iba a dar el fuego a todos.

25 El tlacuache fue una noche a la casa de la vieja y vio que ella descansaba delante de un gran fuego.

—Buenas tardes, señora —dijo el tlacuache—. ¡Ay, qué frío hace! Con su
30 permiso, me gustaría estar un rato al lado del fuego.

La vieja sabía que sí hacía un frío terrible, y le permitió al tlacuache acercarse al fuego. En ese momento el tlacuache puso
35 su **cola** directamente en el fuego y luego salió corriendo de la casa con la cola en llamas para darle el fuego a todas las personas de la región.

Y es por eso que los tlacuaches tienen las
40 colas peladas[5].

---

[4] opossum   [5] hairless

PALABRAS CLAVE
 la cola *tail*

MÁRCALO ⟩ GRAMÁTICA
Circle the verbs in the imperfect tense in the boxed text. Then on the lines below, write the two irregular imperfect verbs.

_____

_____

A pensar...

Number the following events in the correct order. **(Chronological Order)**

_____ Usaba el fuego para cocinar, para luz y calor, y nunca lo compartía.

_____ Hoy, los tlacuaches tienen las colas peladas pero todos tenemos fuego.

_____ Un tlacuache les dijo a los mazatecas que se podía robar el fuego.

_____ Un cometa cayó a la tierra y causó un fuego.

_____ Cuando el tlacuache se acercó al fuego, puso la cola en el fuego.

_____ Con una rama seca, una vieja se llevó el fuego a su casa.

Vocabulario de la lectura

Palabras clave

la cola *tail*
compartir *to share*
la estrella *star*
el fuego *fire*

el miedo *fear*
la piedra *stone, rock*
la rama *branch*
el siglo *century*

A. Answer each question by writing one of the **Palabras clave** in the blank.

1. ¿Hace cuánto tiempo tuvo lugar *(took place)* este cuento? _____

2. ¿Qué se robó el tlacuache? _____

3. ¿De dónde cayó el fuego? _____

4. ¿Qué tenían todos cuando cayó una piedra en llamas a la tierra? _____

5. ¿En qué se llevó el fuego la vieja? _____

B. Write the **Palabras clave** that best complete the sentences.

1. Una _____ en llamas cayó de una _____.

2. Todos tenían _____ y no se acercaban.

3. La vieja se llevó el _____ a su casa en una _____ seca.

4. No quería _____ sus beneficios con nadie.

5. El tlacuache sacrificó la _____ para darle _____ a la humanidad.

¿Comprendiste?

1. ¿Quiénes son los mazatecas?

_____

2. ¿La mujer vieja quería darles fuego a los otros? ¿Por qué?

_____

3. ¿Para qué usaba ella el fuego?

_____

4. ¿Cómo pudo entrar el tlacuache a la casa de la vieja? ¿Qué le dijo?

_____

5. ¿Por qué tienen los tlacuaches la cola sin pelo?

_____

_____

Conexión personal

Myths and legends explain natural phenomena, such as where humanity comes from and why things look the way they do. Think of a natural object or phenomenon whose presence or appearance you can't explain scientifically. Using *El fuego y el tlacuache* as a model, write a brief story to explain this phenomenon.

Title: _____

_____

_____

_____

_____

_____

_____

_____

_____

_____

_____

Para leer   *Los zapotecas y los otavaleños*

Reading Strategy

DRAW A CHART Fill in the chart of the various aspects of the indigenous cultures in Oaxaca and Otavalo. You may make a chart on a separate sheet of paper if you want to include more categories.

Información	Oaxaca	Otavalo
Civilización antigua		
Qué producen ahora		
Ceremonias ancestrales		

What You Need to Know

The Zapotecs are descendants of the Olmec, the ancient Maya, and the Toltec civilizations. Long ago, they believed themselves to have come directly from rocks, trees, and jaguars. Today, the Zapotecs retain much of their heritage, particularly in their customs, dress, songs, and literature. The Otavalo Indians, or *runa,* are descendants of the Cara Indians, who inhabited northern Ecuador about 500 years ago. They were conquered by the Incas first, then by the Spanish. Today, the descendants of these ancient people are skilled textile weavers and are perhaps the most prosperous indigenous group in all of South America.

Los zapotecas y los otavaleños 🎧

La región de Oaxaca tiene base sobre **antiguas** civilizaciones como la zapoteca. Monte Albán, la antigua capital zapoteca, es una zona de ruinas de más de 1.300 años.

5 Allí hay un **campo de pelota,** una gran plaza, un palacio, varios templos y otros **edificios** y estructuras. Todavía hoy, la presencia de los zapotecas es muy **fuerte** en Oaxaca. Hoy continúan la tradición de trabajo en cerámica

10 con técnicas tradicionales: usan, por ejemplo, decoraciones zapotecas auténticas. También, todos los años, los oaxaqueños celebran la Guelaguetza, una ceremonia indígena ancestral. La palabra «guelaguetza» es

15 zapoteca y **quiere decir** «regalo».

Ceremonia de la Guelaguetza

La famosa cerámica oaxaqueña de barro (clay) negro

PALABRAS CLAVE

antiguo(a) *ancient*
el campo de pelota *ball field*
el edificio *building*
fuerte *strong*
querer decir *to mean*

READER'S SUCCESS STRATEGY **Cognates** have the same ancestral language. For Spanish and English, Latin is the common base. For this reason, words in either language derived from Latin are similar. You can easily guess the meanings of Spanish words such as *pasado* or *presente* because they are similar in English.

|||MÁRCALO ⟩ VOCABULARIO
Read the boxed sentence and underline all the cognates. What do you notice about this sentence?

A pensar...

How do the indigenous people in this reading preserve their past? **(Analyze)**

_____

_____

_____

_____

_____

_____

CHALLENGE List the differences and similarities between the Zapotec Indians and the people of Otavalo. **(Compare and Contrast)**

Similarities:

_____

_____

_____

_____

_____

_____

Differences:

_____

_____

_____

_____

_____

_____

20

Una vendedora en un
25 *mercado de textiles,*
Otavalo

El pasado y el présente de los otavaleños es parte esencial del Ecuador moderno. Los indígenas de Otavalo vivían en Ecuador antes del imperio inca y su civilización prospera magníficamente en el presente. Hoy en día, los otavaleños están muy bien organizados comercialmente.

Producen artículos de ropa y de decoración con **tejidos** de colores únicos. Venden estos productos en Ecuador, y también por otros 30 países de Latinoamérica, Estados Unidos y Europa. **Se consideran** internacionalmente un modelo para el progreso económico de los pueblos. También, todavía celebran ceremonias ancestrales. Todos los años, al final 35 del **verano,** celebran la fiesta del Yamor, en honor a la madre tierra[1].

[1] **madre...** mother earth

Hoy muchos otavaleños pueden vender sus artesanías por Internet al mercado internacional.

PALABRAS CLAVE

el tejido *fabric* **el verano** *summer*
considerarse *to be regarded*

Vocabulario de la lectura

Palabras clave

antiguo(a)   *ancient*
el campo de pelota   *ball field*
considerarse   *to be regarded*
el edificio   *building*

fuerte   *strong*
querer decir   *to mean*
el tejido   *fabric*
el verano   *summer*

A. Find the word that relates best to each **Palabra clave.** Write the letter of the word in the blank.

_____ **1.** el tejido

_____ **2.** el verano

_____ **3.** fuerte

_____ **4.** el edificio

_____ **5.** el campo de pelota

a. Superman

b. la ropa está hecha de este material

c. hace calor

d. allí practicaban un deporte ceremonial

e. una casa, por ejemplo

B. Fill in the blanks with the correct forms of **Palabras clave** to complete the paragraph.

Los otavaleños _____ comerciantes excelentes porque venden
                              (1)

sus productos por todo el mundo. Como los otavaleños, los zapotecas

tienen una presencia _____ en su región. Celebran la ceremonia
                               (2)

de la Guelaguetza, que _____ «regalo» y viven cerca de
                                (3)

los _____ que son parte de las _____ruinas de Monte Albán.
         (4)   (5)

¿Comprendiste?

1. ¿Cuál es una de las civilizaciones que son la base de Oaxaca?

_____

_____

2. ¿Qué es Monte Albán? ¿Qué puedes ver en Monte Albán?

_____

_____

3. ¿Cómo puedes ver la presencia de la cultura zapoteca hoy en Oaxaca?

_____

_____

4. ¿Dónde venden los otavaleños los productos que hacen?

_____

_____

5. ¿Qué es el Yamor? ¿Cuándo lo celebran los otavaleños?

_____

_____

Conexión personal

What traditions do you and your family follow that you know came from your ancestors long ago? Write down the traditions you remember and the people you think created them. Share one specific tradition you are especially fond of.

My Favorite Traditions

Tradition _____

Who started it? _____

Tradition _____

Who started it? _____

Tradition _____

Who started it? _____

My favorite: _____

_____

_____

_____

Para leer   *Dos odas de Pablo Neruda*

Reading Strategy

MAKE A COMPARISON CHART In this chart, list four images or metaphors per ode. Compare them by (a) meaning and (b) impact on you. Which are your favorites?

	sal	aceite
1	canta con una boca ahogada por la tierra	
2		
3		
4		

What You Need to Know

Pablo Neruda, who took on that pen name because his Chilean family did not approve of his literary leanings, was a writer, diplomat, senator, and political activist as well as a poet. During his later years, he was recognized on numerous occasions: he received several important international peace prizes and finally the Nobel Prize for Literature in 1971. Neruda has been called the "people's poet" because his central theme was the struggle for social justice. His wonderfully varied work touched on many other themes, such as love poems and odes to everyday objects.

READER'S SUCCESS STRATEGY A poet uses many forms of imagery to portray his ideas. One of the most important is personification, which gives human characteristics to abstract ideas or things. Notice how Neruda personifies salt in *"Oda a la sal."*

MÁRCALO **GRAMÁTICA**
Neruda makes you feel the intensity of his observation when he speaks in past tense. In the boxed verses, circle the three verbs in the preterit form.

Dos odas de Pablo Neruda

Pablo Neruda (1904–1973) fue un famoso poeta chileno (Premio Nobel de Literatura, 1971). Neruda escribió muchas odas[1]. En sus odas, Neruda describe las cosas más básicas de la vida[2]. Por ejemplo, escribió una oda a la mesa y otra a la silla, objetos que usamos todos los días. También escribió odas a muchos alimentos[3] esenciales como la cebolla, el limón, la sal y el aceite. Lee los siguientes versos de Neruda.

Oda a la sal

Esta sal
del salero[4]
yo la vi en los salares[5].
Sé que
no van a creerme,
pero
canta,
canta la sal, la **piel**
de los salares,
canta
con una **boca** ahogada[6]
por la tierra[7].
Me estremecí en aquellas
soledades[8]
cuando **escuché**
la voz[9]
de
la sal
en el desierto...

[1] odes [2] life [3] food items [4] saltshaker [5] salt mines
[6] stifled [7] earth [8] lonely places [9] voice

PALABRAS CLAVE
cantar *to sing*
la piel *skin*
la boca *mouth*

estremecerse *to shudder*
escuchar *to hear*

Olivar en Extremadura, España

Oda al aceite

...allí
en
los secos[1]
olivares[2], [...]
la cápsula
perfecta
de la oliva
llenando
con sus constelaciones el follaje[3]:
más tarde
las **vasijas**,
el milagro[4],
el aceite. [...]
Aceite, [...]
llave celeste de la mayonesa,
suave y **sabroso**
sobre las lechugas, [...]
Aceite, [...]
eres idioma
castellano[5]:
hay sílabas de aceite,
hay palabras
útiles[6] y olorosas[7]
como tu fragante materia...

---

[1] dry   [2] olive groves   [3] foliage   [4] miracle
[5] **idioma...** Spanish language   [6] useful   [7] fragrant

CHALLENGE Why do you think Neruda equates oil to words and language, and especially to the Spanish language? **(Infer)**

PALABRAS CLAVE

el aceite *oil*   **la llave** *key*
llenar *to fill*   **sabroso(a)** *tasty*
la vasija *container*

Vocabulario de la lectura

Palabras clave

el aceite *oil*   la llave *key*

la boca *mouth*   **llenar** *to fill*

cantar *to sing*   **la piel** *skin*

escuchar *to hear*   sabroso(a) *tasty*

estremecerse *to shudder*   **la vasija** *container*

A. Usando la lista de **Palabras clave,** llena cada espacio en blanco con una palabra relacionada.

    1. botella   _____

    2. delicioso   _____

    3. música   _____

    4. oír   _____

    5. completar   _____

B. Escribe la forma correcta de la **Palabra clave** que mejor complete cada oración.

    1. Si tomamos el sol, le debemos poner bloqueador a

       nuestra _____.

    2. Usamos _____ para comer o para hablar.

    3. Anoche _____ durante la película porque me dio mucho miedo.

    4. Le ponemos _____ a una ensalada.

    5. Necesitamos _____ para abrir la puerta.

¿Comprendiste?

1. ¿Quién es Pablo Neruda? ¿Qué hace Neruda en sus poemas?

_____

2. Según Neruda, ¿qué hace la sal? ¿Dónde puedes «escuchar» la sal?

_____

3. ¿De qué tipo de aceite escribe Neruda?

_____

4. ¿Con qué cosas compara el aceite?

_____

_____

Conexión personal

Using Neruda's poems as models, write an ode to a food you eat often. Try to include details and comparisons that appeal to more than one sense. Use the graphic organizer to get you started.

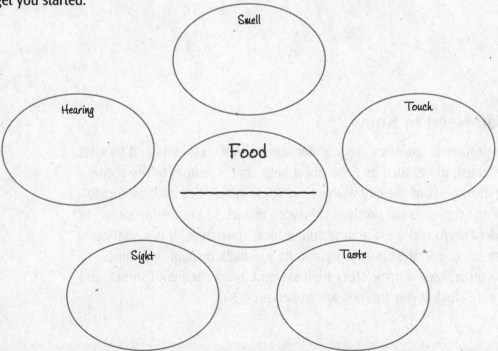

Para leer   *Dos tradiciones culinarias*

Reading Strategy

USE A MIND MAP FOR COMPARISONS Add onto this mind map
to provide all the facts about the traditional restaurants and foods
found in Madrid and Montevideo. Add as many circles as you can.

What You Need to Know

Madrid's restaurants and bars are popular among both residents and tourists.
Historic establishments such as *Casa Botín* help attract visitors to the scenic
older neighborhoods of the city where they enjoy specialties such as *cocido
madrileño* and *tapas,* small portions of savory dishes. In Montevideo, the
Mercado del Puerto is the place to taste the local specialties. It is a soaring
structure made of metal, stone, and glass. As you walk through grandiose
iron gates you will see a three-story-high skylight, blackened with smoke and
age. Its ornate clock tower's hands are frozen on 4:30.

Dos tradiciones culinarias 🎧

El restaurante madrileño Sobrino de Botín

El cordero asado con verduras, un plato típico madrileño

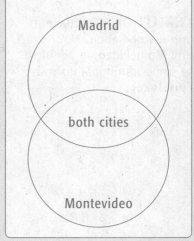

El cocido madrileño es la comida más típica de Madrid. Este **guiso** es de **garbanzos**, diferentes **verduras** y **carnes**. Se hierve en agua y
5 se sirve en tres platos separados, o vuelcos: la sopa, las verduras con los garbanzos, y la carne. Estos platos forman la base del típico menú madrileño. El mejor lugar para probar un menú madrileño es el restaurante Sobrino
10 de Botín. Este restaurante se abrió en el año 1725. Está en un edificio del año 1590 y queda en un barrio histórico, en la calle de los Cuchilleros, cerca de la Plaza Mayor. Según el Libro Guinness de los récords, la Casa Botín,
15 como también se conoce, es el restaurante más antiguo del mundo. En la Casa Botín sirven platos tradicionales de carne como el cochinillo[1] asado y el cordero[2] asado. Es un restaurante favorito de muchos españoles.

---
[1] suckling pig   [2] lamb

PALABRAS CLAVE
el guiso *stew*
el garbanzo *chick pea, garbanzo bean*
las verduras *vegetables*
la carne *meat*

READING TIP In this reading, you will see the impersonal **se.** It is used to describe things that get done when the subject, or the person doing an action, is unknown or unimportant. The phrase **se hierve en agua** is an example of the impersonal **se.**

▥▥ **MÁRCALO** ⟩ **GRAMÁTICA**
Read the boxed text and look for sentences where the impersonal **se** is used. Circle three verbs that use the impersonal **se**.

READER'S SUCCESS STRATEGY Use a Venn diagram to help you compare and contrast the typical foods of Madrid and Montevideo. Copy the Venn diagram below onto a larger sheet of paper and jot down facts about Madrid, Montevideo, and both cities.

Madrid

both cities

Montevideo

_____
_____
_____
_____
_____
_____
_____
_____

CHALLENGE What have you learned about Madrid and Montevideo, in addition to some traditional dishes? (**Analyze**)

_____
_____
_____
_____
_____
_____
_____
_____

Un restaurante en Colonia del Sacramento, una ciudad en la costa de Uruguay

Un plato con tomate y mariscos

20 Pero también muchos turistas lo visitan todos los días.

La carne, el **pescado** y los mariscos[3] 25 son los **alimentos** básicos de la región donde queda Montevideo. La **parrillada** (carne asada en una parrilla) es el plato de carne tradicional de la región. Como[4] Montevideo queda en la costa, el 30 pescado y los mariscos siempre están muy accesibles y son, por eso[5], los otros alimentos básicos. Un lugar muy especial para ir a comer parrilladas, pescado y mariscos en Montevideo es el Mercado del Puerto. El 35 Mercado del Puerto se construyó en 1868. Es grande y muy bello: está hecho de metal, de piedra y de **vidrio**. Generalmente, la gente va al Mercado del Puerto para almorzar, no para cenar; muy pocos restaurantes están abiertos 40 para la cena.

_____

[3] shellfish   [4] Since   [5] **por...** therefore

PALABRAS CLAVE

el pescado *fish*   **la parrillada** *grilled meat, barbecue*
el alimento *food*   **el vidrio** *glass*

Vocabulario de la lectura

Palabras clave

el alimento *food*
la carne *meat*
el garbanzo *chick pea, garbanzo bean*
el guiso *stew*

la parrillada *grilled meat, barbecue*
el pescado *fish*
las verduras *vegetables*
el vidrio *glass*

A. Tacha *(Cross out)* la palabra que no esté relacionada con las otras.

1. vidrio, pescado, alimento

2. verduras, garbanzo, pescado

3. madera, guiso, vidrio

4. cocido, parrillada, garbanzo

5. carne, verduras, zanahoria

B. Estás comiendo en un nuevo restaurante español. Completa cada pregunta con una de las **Palabras clave.**

1. ¿_____ viene del océano Pacífico?

2. ¿Qué tipos de carne asada hay en _____?

3. ¿Sirven la carne con zanahorias y otras _____?

4. ¿Sirven _____ como el cocido madrileño?

5. ¿Todos _____ que sirven son frescos?

¿Comprendiste?

1. ¿Cuál es una especialidad de Madrid?

_____

_____

2. ¿En qué restaurante de Madrid puedes ir a comer platos madrileños?

_____

3. ¿Cuáles son dos productos que comen mucho en Montevideo?

_____

4. ¿Cuándo construyeron el Mercado del Puerto?

_____

5. ¿Cuál es una comida básica de España y Uruguay?

_____

Conexión personal

What is a favorite typical dish of your region or town? Write the ingredients of the dish and some notes on how it is prepared.

_____

_____

_____

_____

_____

_____

Para leer   *La casa de los espíritus*

Reading Strategy

To help you manage this complex passage, try to restate each paragraph in a few short phrases or sentences as you go along. If you are having trouble, go back and reread, jotting down notes or questions. Complete your notes on a separate sheet of paper.

Primer párrafo:

1. Clara decidió no hablar. _____

_____

_____

2. _____

_____

_____

3. _____

_____

_____

What You Need to Know

This reading is a short excerpt from the novel *La casa de los espíritus (The House of the Spirits)* by Isabel Allende. Originally published in Spain in 1982, it tells the tale of several generations of one family in Chile. In the book, Allende uses a mixture of magical and realistic elements and a multi-generational plot to tell her compelling story. The novel follows three generations of strong women as they struggle against a domineering family patriarch. As a political backdrop, a growing conflict between opposing forces in the country culminates in a military coup. While Chile is never named, the plot reflects the history of the author's homeland. This reading introduces Clara, one of the book's main characters.

La casa de los espíritus

La película estadounidense The House of the Spirits (1993) *es una adaptación de la primera novela de la escritora chilena Isabel Allende,* La casa de los espíritus. *En estos fragmentos, conocemos a Clara, un personaje importante del libro.*

Clara tenía diez años cuando decidió que no valía la pena
5 hablar y se encerró en el mutismo[1].
Su vida[2] cambió

notablemente. El médico de la familia, el gordo y afable doctor Cuevas, intentó curarle
10 el silencio con píldoras[3] de su invención, con vitaminas en jarabe[4] y tocaciones de miel[5] de bórax en la **garganta** pero sin ningún resultado aparente [...]

---

[1] **se...** shut herself into silence   [2] life   [3] pills   [4] syrup
[5] **tocaciones...** applications of honey-based remedy

PALABRAS CLAVE
 la película   *movie, film*
 la garganta   *throat*

La nana tenía la idea
15 de que un buen **susto**
podía conseguir que la
niña hablara[6] y se pasó
nueve años inventando
recursos desesperados
20 para aterrorizar[7] a Clara,
con lo cual sólo **consiguió**
inmunizarla contra la
sorpresa y el **espanto**. Al poco tiempo Clara
no tenía miedo de nada [...]

25   La pequeña Clara **leía** mucho. Su
interés por la lectura era indiscriminado y
le daban lo mismo[8] los libros mágicos de los
baúles encantados[9] de su tío Marcos, que los
documentos del Partido Liberal que su padre
30 **guardaba** en su estudio. Llenaba incontables[10]
cuadernos con anotaciones[11] privadas, donde
fueron quedando
registrados[12] los
acontecimientos
35 de ese tiempo, que
gracias a eso no **se**
perdieron borrados
por la neblina del
olvido[13], y ahora yo puedo usarlos para
40 rescatar[14] su memoria [...]

---

[6] **podía...** would make the girl talk again   [7] terrify, frighten
[8] **le...** they were the same to her   [9] **baúles...** magical chests
[10] countless   [11] annotations, entries
[12] **fueron...** were being recorded
[13] **borrados...** erased by the fog of oblivion   [14] rescue

PALABRAS CLAVE

el susto	*fright, scare*	**leer**	*to read*
el recurso	*way*	**guardar**	*to keep*
conseguir	*to manage to, succeed in*	**el acontecimiento**	*event, happening*
el espanto	*terror, fright*	**perderse**	*to become lost*

What do you think of **la nana's** attempts to scare Clara into talking? Why do you think the author included this passage? **(Evaluate, Analyze)**

CHALLENGE Read the last sentence in the passage. Who do you think narrates the novel? What might her purpose be? **(Infer)**

Vocabulario de la lectura

Palabras clave

el acontecimiento *event, happening*
conseguir *to manage to, succeed in*
el espanto *terror, fright*
la garganta *throat*
guardar *to keep*

leer *to read*
la película *movie, film*
perderse *to become lost*
el recurso *way*
el susto *fright, scare*

A. Escribe la **Palabra clave** que esté relacionada con cada palabra o frase.

1. película de horror   _____

2. una cosa que pasa   _____

3. necesitar un mapa   _____

4. el cine   _____

5. parte del cuerpo   _____

B. Escribe la **Palabra clave** que mejor complete cada oración.

1. Jorge, ¿_____ hablar con la actriz de la película?

2 Trato todos los _____ para estar saludable.

3. Cuando era niño _____ muchos cuentos.

4. Su memoria _____ todos sus recuerdos;
   nunca olvida nada.

5. Todos los días ocurren muchos _____ en todo
   el mundo.

¿Comprendiste?

1. ¿Quién es la autora de *La casa de los espíritus?* ¿De dónde es?

_____

2. ¿Cómo es el personaje de Clara?

_____

3. ¿Qué le pasa a Clara a los diez años?

_____

4. ¿Por qué le pierde Clara el miedo a todo?

_____

5. ¿Qué cosas le ayudan a Clara a recordar en la vida?

_____

Conexión personal

What novel would you like to see made into a film? Sketch out a plan for a film based on the novel. Remember that when you make a movie based on a novel, you have to cut some of the material from the book. List the key scenes from the novel that you would use in your movie.

Novela: _____

_____

_____

_____

_____

_____

_____

_____

_____

_____

Para leer   *El Óscar y el Ariel*

Reading Strategy

COMPARE OSCAR AND ARIEL Use this Venn diagram to compare the two great prizes, the Oscar and the Ariel. In the center, write down *similarities.* In the non-overlapping parts of the circles, write down *differences.* Make sure you have included all key information.

Óscar   Ariel

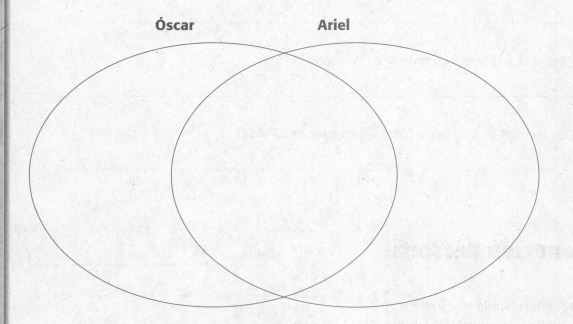

What You Need to Know

Mexican cinema goes back to the beginning of the 20th century when early filmmakers shot footage of the Mexican Revolution and other events. But it was in the 1930s that Mexican film began to take off, culminating in the "golden age" of the 1940s, when the Mexican cinema had the same glamour as Hollywood in that period. The industry suffered a decline in the 1960s, but since then has been reborn and become more vital than ever. More recent films, such as *Como agua para chocolate,* became international hits that drew large audiences in the United States as well as in the Spanish-speaking world.

El Óscar y el Ariel:
dos premios prestigiosos

Todo el mundo conoce el Óscar, el premio de la Academia de Hollywood. Pero

5 no todos conocen su simbolismo e historia.

Ceremonia del Óscar, Los Ángeles

La estatuilla[1] representa a un **caballero**

10 con una **espada**, sobre un **carrete** de película de cinco radios[2]. Los radios simbolizan las cinco profesiones originales de la Academia: los actores, los **guionistas,** los directores, los productores y los técnicos.

15 En su origen, «Óscar» era solamente un **sobrenombre** que inició Margaret Herrick, la **bibliotecaria** de la Academia; decía que la estatuilla del caballero era como su tío Óscar. Luego, otros empezaron a referirse a la

20 estatuilla y al premio como «el Óscar».

El primer premio fue **otorgado** en 1929. El puertorriqueño José Ferrer fue el primer actor hispano que recibió el Óscar de Mejor Actor, en el año 1950, por su papel

25 en *Cyrano de Bergerac*. Rita Moreno, también

---

[1] statuette   [2] spokes

PALABRAS CLAVE
el caballero *knight*
la espada *sword*
el carrete *reel*
el (la) guionista *scriptwriter*

el sobrenombre *nickname*
el (la) bibliotecario(a) *librarian*
otorgar *to award*

READER'S SUCCESS STRATEGY Before reading the text, look at the title, pictures, and captions to help you figure out how it is organized. Knowing a little about the passage beforehand will help you better understand what it's about. It can also help you locate specific information.

A pensar...

Which films won the most recent Oscars? Do you think they were the best choices to represent U.S. cinema? Why or why not? **(Connect, Activate Associated Knowledge)**

In Unit 5, you studied double
object pronouns. Look through
the boxed text and circle the
double object pronoun. To what
does each of the pronouns
refer?

CHALLENGE Why are awards
like the Oscar and the Ariel
important to cinema? What
purpose do they serve? **(Make
Judgments)**

puertorriqueña, fue la primera actriz hispana
en ganar el premio por su papel en *West Side
Story* en 1961.

30 En México, el premio nacional de cine
es el Ariel. Se lo otorga la Academia Mexicana
de Artes y Ciencias Cinematográficas a las
estrellas de cine mexicano cada **primavera.**
Como el Óscar, la estatuilla del Ariel es
simbólica. El hombre alado[3] representa la
35 libertad del espíritu y del arte, un deseo de
ascender[4] y también la unidad de la cultura
hispanoamericana.

La Academia se creó[5] durante la «Época
de Oro» en los años 40. El cine mexicano
40 prosperaba con un grupo de grandes estrellas,
como María Félix, Dolores del Río, Pedro
Infante y Cantinflas (Mario Moreno). Hoy día,
la Academia reconoce[6] a los mejores del cine
con los premios Ariel en el Palacio de Bellas
45 Artes en la Ciudad de México.

---

[3] winged   [4] **deseo...** desire to soar
[5] was created   [6] recognizes

PALABRAS CLAVE
la primavera *spring*

Vocabulario de la lectura

Palabras clave

el (la) bibliotecario(a) *librarian*

el caballero *knight*

el carrete *reel*

la espada *sword*

el (la) guionista *scriptwriter*

otorgar *to award*

la primavera *spring*

el sobrenombre *nickname*

A. ¿Qué **Palabra clave** corresponde a cada una de las siguientes definiciones?

1. Es un objeto circular: _____

2. Estación del año: _____

3. Persona que cuida y busca libros: _____

4. Persona que monta a caballo y lucha *(fights)* con dragones: _____

5. Arma del caballero: _____

B. Escribe la forma correcta de la **Palabra clave** que mejor complete cada oración.

1. No pueden hacer una película sin _____.

2. «Óscar» era originalmente el _____ de la estatuilla de la Academia.

3. La Academia le _____ el premio de mejor actriz cuatro veces a Katharine Hepburn.

4. El tío de _____ de la Academia se llamaba Óscar.

5. Cada año, en la _____, la Academia Mexicana de Artes y Ciencias Cinematográficas otorga los Arieles.

¿Comprendiste?

1. ¿Cuáles son las cinco profesiones de la Academia de Hollywood?

_____

2. ¿Cuándo empezaron a dar el premio Óscar? ¿Quiénes fueron los primeros hispanos en recibir el premio?

_____

_____

3. ¿En qué década crearon la Academia Mexicana?

_____

4. ¿Qué representa Ariel?

_____

_____

Conexión personal

What movie do you think should win an Oscar this year? Give the reasons why you think it deserves an Academy Award.

La mejor película del año

_____

_____

_____

_____

_____

_____

_____

_____

_____

_____

Para leer   *¡Ayúdame, Paulina!*

Reading Strategy

SUMMARIZE IDEAS AND ADD YOUR OWN Complete the three conversation boxes, one to summarize Neomi's written request, one for Paulina's response, and one for your own response. What do you think Neomi should do?

Neomi

Su problema: _____

Causa del problema: _____

Su reacción al problema: _____

Paulina

Su Solución: _____
Por qué y cómo puede
ayudar a Neomi _____

Yo

Mi Solución: _____
Por qué y cómo puedo
ayudar a Neomi _____

What You Need to Know

Advice columns have been a staple of newspapers and magazines in the United States and throughout the Spanish-speaking world for decades. Some U.S. papers print advice columns for their Spanish-speaking audiences. The *Dallas Morning News,* for example, features *Consejos,* a bicultural advice column for young people. In this reading, you will see what Paulina Pensativa has to say to a teen who is struggling at her new school.

A pensar...

What do you think is the cause of Neomi's problems? (**Draw Conclusions**)

_____

_____

_____

_____

_____

_____

_____

_____

_____

_____

_____

_____

_____

¡Ayúdame, Paulina!

Este artículo es de la página de opiniones y **consejos** de un **periódico.** Una estudiante presenta un problema y busca los consejos. Luego, la escritora Paulina Pensativa le responde.

Querida Paulina
Consejos para los jóvenes de hoy

POR PAULINA PENSATIVA

QUERIDA PAULINA: Me llamo Neomi. Tengo quince años y vivo en Salcedo. El verano pasado, mi familia y yo **nos mudamos** aquí de Santo Domingo. En mi **liceo** de antes, era muy estudiosa. Iba a todas mis clases, siempre hacía la tarea y sacaba buenas notas. Me gustaban todas las **materias.** También tenía buenas amigas y practicaba deportes.

Pero después de mudarme aquí, algo cambió. En mi nuevo liceo, las clases ya no me interesan. Me encuentro[1] muy aburrida en el **aula** y sin ganas de estudiar. A veces no estoy de acuerdo con lo que dicen los maestros, y no les escucho bien. Para mí es difícil no sólo ir al liceo, sino también quedarme allí por todo el día.

Hace poco tiempo, dejé de hacer la tarea y de ir a algunas clases. Ahora estoy empezando a **reprobar** materias. Los maestros me dicen que si no vuelvo a estudiar, voy a tener que repetir curso[2]. Por eso pienso dejar el liceo.

Lo único que me interesa es el arte. Soy artística y me encanta dibujar. Prefiero pasar el día dibujando un retrato, no tomando un examen. Pero mis padres dicen que es importante que yo me quede en el liceo. No sé qué hacer. ¡Ayúdame, por favor!

[1] **Me...** I find myself
[2] **repetir...** to repeat a grade

PALABRAS CLAVE
el consejo _advice_
el periódico _newspaper_
mudarse _to move_
el liceo _high school_

la materia _school subject_
el aula (f.) _classroom_
reprobar _to fail_

EL DIARIO QUISQUEYANO

QUERIDA NEOMI: Me parece que todavía no estás adaptada[3] a tu nuevo liceo. Antes estabas contenta entre todas las personas que conocías. Todavía no conoces ni el lugar donde te encuentras ni a la gente que son tus compañeros. Es necesario que seas paciente. Te vas a adaptar; es una cuestión de tiempo.

Sin embargo, si no te gustan las clases, es bueno que hables con tus maestros. Explícales tu punto de vista, y **te aseguro** que ellos te van a escuchar. Tal vez enseñan cosas que ya aprendiste. Los maestros están abiertos a tus opiniones sobre lo que quieres aprender.

También, si tu pasión es el arte, ¿por qué no tomas una clase adicional? Si estudias lo que te interesa, puede ayudar tu autoestima[4] y aumentar[5] tu interés en otras materias. ¡Ojalá que haya una escuela de bellas artes en Salcedo que puedas investigar!

Tus padres tienen razón. Es importante que no dejes el liceo. Por un lado, hay que tomar tiempo para adaptarte. Por otro lado, debes hacer todo lo que puedas para estar contenta con tus estudios. Dijiste que eras buena estudiante. Yo digo que todavía lo eres. ¡Suerte!

[3] adjusted
[4] self-esteem
[5] to increase

READING TIP In Spanish, double negatives are grammatically correct, and often required. Here, the triple negative **Todavía... no [conoces]... ni... ni** is used to convey "neither... nor."

MÁRCALO GRAMÁTICA
You have learned how to use the subjunctive and recognize it after expressions of hope and impersonal expressions. Look through the boxed text and circle the verbs in the subjunctive mood.

CHALLENGE Do you agree with Paulina's advice? If so, what other suggestions would you make to Neomi? If not, write your own response to Neomi.

_____

_____

_____

_____

_____

_____

_____

_____

_____

_____

_____

PALABRAS CLAVE
sin embargo *however*   **asegurar** *to assure*

Vocabulario de la lectura

Palabras clave

asegurar *to assure*
el aula (f.) *classroom*
el consejo *advice*
el liceo *high school*
la materia *school subject*

mudarse *to move*
el periódico *newspaper*
reprobar *to fail*
sin embargo *however*

A. Llena cada espacio en blanco con una **Palabra clave** que esté relacionada.

1. sala de clase _____

2. escuela secundaria _____

3. matemáticas _____

4. leer _____

5. sugerencia _____

B. Paloma tiene un problema. Lee su carta y llena cada espacio en blanco con la forma correcta de una **Palabra clave.**

Querida Paulina:

El año pasado mi mamá y yo _____ a Las Vegas. Todavía no
(1)

tengo buenos amigos. Mi nuevo _____ es muy grande; tiene
(2)

más de mil estudiantes. No me gustan las _____ que llevo,
(3)

excepto las ciencias. Mi mamá _____ que todo saldrá
(4)

bien *(will turn out)* si tengo un poco de paciencia. _____, no
(5)

creo que tenga la paciencia necesaria.

¡Necesito _____!
(6)

¿Comprendiste?

1. ¿Quién es Paulina?

_____

2. ¿Por qué piensa Neomi dejar el liceo?

_____

_____

3. ¿Qué dicen sus padres sobre su problema?

_____

4. Nombra *(name)* tres cosas que Paulina dice para ayudarla.

_____

_____

5. ¿Cómo era Neomi en su liceo de antes?

_____

Conexión personal

What advice would you give to your favorite celebrity or character from a book or movie? You are a writer of an advice column and this person has written to you for help. Write your response.

Querido(a) _____

_____

_____

_____

_____

_____

_____

_____

_____

_____

_____

Para leer   *Los padrinos*

Reading Strategy

CHART THE TRADITION Use the chart to understand the tradition of *padrinos* in Latin America. List key information about *padrinos* and their role.

Información clave	Padrinos de boda	Padrinos de bautizo
Quiénes son		
Su papel		
Cómo ayudan a una familia		

What You Need to Know

The terms *compadre* and *comadre* define the very special relationship between the parents and godparents of a child. There is no precise translation for this close bond. *Comadres* or *compadres* are people you would trust with your life and that of your child. The words *comadre* and *compadre* are also sometimes used to describe an especially close friendship between two people who do not share the tie of godparenthood. Whether or not they are godparents to each other's children, however, *comadres* and *compadres* consider themselves friends for life.

Los padrinos

Los padrinos de boda tienen un papel importante.

En los países latinoamericanos existen dos tipos de padrinos:

5 los **padrinos** de **boda** y los padrinos de **bautizo**.

En Paraguay, como en muchos otros países de Latinoamérica, cuando dos novios

10 se casan, éstos **escogen** a un hombre y a una mujer como los padrinos para su boda. A diferencia de las bodas estadounidenses en que los novios generalmente escogen a sus mejores amigos o hermanos para ser los testigos[1],

15 o *best man* y *maid of honor,* en los países latinoamericanos, el padrino y la madrina son los testigos principales y casi siempre son una **pareja casada.** Normalmente uno de ellos es **pariente** o del novio o de la novia.

20 La función de los padrinos de boda no termina con la ceremonia de matrimonio. Los padrinos tienen un papel muy importante en la vida familiar. **Comparten** los momentos más importantes de la vida de los esposos.

---

[1] witnesses

PALABRAS CLAVE
los padrinos (el padrino,
   la madrina) *godparents*
   (godfather, godmother)
la boda *wedding*
el bautizo *baptism, christening*

escoger *to choose*
la pareja *couple, pair*
casado(a) *married*
el (la) pariente *relative*
compartir *to share*

READING TIP When you read articles or other materials that compare and contrast cultural traditions, look out for terms such as **a diferencia de,** which signal that two things are being contrasted.

READER'S SUCCESS STRATEGY After you read each paragraph, jot down a few notes so that you can figure out and remember the main ideas of the text and how it is organized.

A pensar...

Compare and contrast the role of **padrinos de boda** in a couple's life with the roles of the best man and maid of honor. **(Compare and Contrast)**

_____

_____

_____

_____

_____

_____

_____

_____

_____

_____

_____

You have just learned about family relationships in Spanish. Circle the family relationship words in the boxed text.

CHALLENGE In your own words, describe the role of **los padrinos** in the life of a child. (Paraphrase)

_____

_____

_____

_____

_____

_____

_____

_____

_____

_____

_____

_____

_____

_____

_____

_____

_____

_____

Unos padrinos orgullosos con su ahijado

25   Antes del **nacimiento** de un niño, muchos padres dominicanos, como en otras partes de Latinoamérica, escogen a los padrinos de su futuro hijo. Los padrinos pueden ser parientes o amigos de los padres.

30 Muchas veces éstos son los padrinos de la boda, especialmente en el caso del primer hijo del matrimonio. Es en el momento del bautizo del niño cuando los padrinos y los padres se convierten en[2] compadres.

35   Los padrinos sirven como segundos padres para el niño, o el **ahijado.** Si los padres no pueden continuar cuidando[3] a su hijo, los compadres se hacen cargo de criarlo[4]. Están presentes en muchas fiestas

40 familiares y ocasiones importantes, como los cumpleaños y las graduaciones escolares.

     Como vemos, el papel de los padrinos es muy especial, y la relación entre ellos y sus ahijados es una parte integral de la cultura

45 latinoamericana.

---

[2] become   [3] taking care of
[4] **se hacen…** they take charge of raising him

PALABRAS CLAVE
el nacimiento *birth*   el (la) ahijado(a) *godchild (godson, goddaughter)*

Vocabulario de la lectura

Palabras clave

el (la) ahijado(a) *godchild*
   (godson, goddaughter)
el bautizo *baptism, christening*
la boda *wedding*
casado(a) *married*
compartir *to share*

escoger *to choose*
el nacimiento *birth*
los padrinos (el padrino, la madrina)
   godparent (godfather, godmother)
la pareja *couple, pair*
el (la) pariente *relative*

A. Llena cada espacio en blanco con un antónimo o palabra opuesta de la lista de **Palabras clave.**

1. muerte _____

2. madrina _____

3. soltera _____

4. divorcio _____

5. uno, individuo _____

B. Escribe la **Palabra clave** que mejor complete cada oración.

1. Amigos, parientes y padrinos fueron al _____ del bebé en la iglesia San Lorenzo.

2. Los padres _____ un nombre bello para el muchacho: Javier.

3. Mi _____ favorito es mi tío Javier.

4. Paco y Mariluz son buenos padrinos; van a cada fiesta de cumpleaños

   de sus _____.

5. Los padrinos de boda _____ los momentos importantes de la vida de la pareja casada.

¿Comprendiste?

1. ¿Quiénes son los padrinos en las bodas paraguayas?

_____

2. ¿Por qué son importantes los padrinos después de la boda?

_____

3. Generalmente, ¿quiénes son los padrinos de un bautizo?

_____

_____

4. Si los padres no pueden cuidar a su hijo, ¿qué papel toman los compadres?

_____

5. ¿Cuándo se convierten los padres y los padrinos en compadres?

_____

Conexión personal

What qualities would you want in a person you might consider your *compadre* or *comadre?* Fill in the word web with words or phrases that describe what this ideal friend would be like. On a separate sheet of paper, write a description of your dream *compadre* or *comadre.* Do you know such a person now?

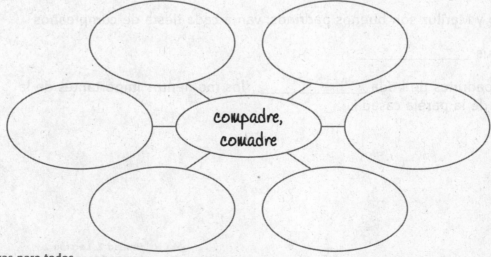

compadre, comadre

Para leer   *Sitio Web: Fundación Bello Ecuador*

Reading Strategy

MAKE A MIND MAP Complete the mind map showing the objective and the programs of the **Fundación Bello Ecuador** *(FBE)*. Add as many details as you can with circles and lines.

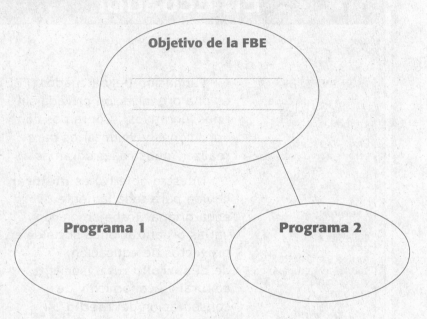

Objetivo de la FBE

Programa 1   Programa 2

What You Need to Know

With the growth of the Internet, the nonprofit world has been able to market itself much more easily. With a simple search, you can locate thousands of charities around the globe. You can make a donation, get more information, or sign up to volunteer with the click of a mouse. In this reading, you will explore the types of information you might find on a nonprofit organization's Web site.

CHALLENGE You are trying to convince someone to make a donation to **Fundación Bello Ecuador.** In one or two sentences, summarize the organization's mission. **(Summarize)**

Sitio Web: Fundación Bello Ecuador

http://www.fbe.org.ec

Programas De Voluntarios En Ecuador

Información y programas   Cómo **ayudarnos**   Formulario[1] para programas   Galería de fotos   Contáctenos

Otros **enlaces:**

Clases de quechua y otros **idiomas** indígenas

Entrenamiento[5] en temas ecológicos

Información general sobre Ecuador

¡Nuevo! Participa en proyecto cultural y económico en los Andes y aprende sobre las culturas y artesanías indígenas.

Haz clic aquí para más información

Fundación Bello Ecuador (FBE) es una organización privada sin fines lucrativos[2]. Contamos con[3] donaciones y voluntarios para realizar[4] nuestros programas.

Nuestro objetivo es **mejorar** la vida para toda la gente ecuatoriana. Trabajamos con varias organizaciones sociales en proyectos de educación, de **desarrollo** rural, social, cultural y económico y de conservación del **medio ambiente.**

[1] application form
[2] **sin...** non-profit
[3] **Contamos...** We count on
[4] to fulfill, make happen
[5] Training

PALABRAS CLAVE
ayudar *to help*
el enlace *link*
el idioma *language*

mejorar *to improve*
el desarrollo *development*
el medio ambiente *environment*

http://www.fbe.org.ec

Programas De Voluntarios En Ecuador

Información y programas | Cómo ayudarnos | Formulario para programas | Galería de fotos | Contáctenos

Otros enlaces:

Clases de quechua y otros idiomas indígenas

Entrenamiento en temas ecológicos

Información general sobre Ecuador

¡Nuevo! Participa en proyecto cultural y económico en los Andes y aprende sobre las culturas y artesanías indígenas.

Haz clic aquí para más información

Aquí hay algunos de los trabajos que ofrecemos

Programas de reforestación y conservación de plantas amazónicas: Trabaja en las **selvas** y los jardines botánicos.

Investigaciones biológicas y programas de protección de especies en peligro de extinción: Ayuda a investigar los problemas de los animales de la selva amazónica o en las Galápagos. También ayuda a **buscarles** soluciones.

Programas de educación sobre el medio ambiente: Da clases de biología, ecología, conservación y reciclaje a niños y adultos de varias comunidades.

Programas de desarrollo rural: Trabaja en el campo para la construcción de escuelas y el desarrollo de la infraestructura y el sistema de agricultura.

Programas de salud: Trabaja en clínicas y hospitales o en programas de educación sobre la salud.

PALABRAS CLAVE

la selva *jungle*
el peligro *danger*

buscar *to look for*
la salud *health*

A pensar...

1. What kinds of convictions and beliefs would a volunteer for **Fundación Bello Ecuador** probably have? **(Make Judgments)**

_____

_____

_____

_____

_____

_____

_____

2. If you were to volunteer to work in Ecuador, what language or languages would be useful to know? **(Draw Conclusions)**

_____

_____

_____

_____

_____

_____

_____

MÁRCALO VOCABULARIO

By now, you know how to use cognates to help you understand unfamiliar readings. Circle the cognates in the boxed text.

Vocabulario de la lectura

Palabras clave

ayudar *to help*   **el medio ambiente** *environment*

buscar *to look for*   **mejorar** *to improve*

el desarrollo *development*   **el peligro** *danger*

el enlace *link*   **la salud** *health*

el idioma *language*   **la selva** *jungle*

A. Para cada palabra de la primera columna, busca la definición en la segunda columna. Escribe la letra de la definición correcta en el espacio en blanco.

_____ **1.** mejorar   a. El objetivo de esto es localizar o encontrar.

_____ **2.** enlace   b. Es el estado general del cuerpo.

_____ **3.** medio ambiente   c. «Perfeccionar» es un sinónimo.

_____ **4.** buscar   d. «La naturaleza» es un sinónimo.

_____ **5.** salud   e. Esto conecta o une las cosas.

B. Escribe las **Palabras clave** que completen las oraciones.

1. Muchos animales están en _____ de extinción.

2. Las _____ amazónicas son bellas.

3. Muy pocos hablan quechua, un _____ indígena.

4. El _____ de la economía en países del tercer mundo es importante.

5. ¿Quieren _____ a proteger el medio ambiente? Háganse socios de organizaciones como el World Wildlife Fund.

¿Comprendiste?

1. ¿Cuál es el objetivo de esta organización?

_____

2. Si a alguien le interesa enseñar, ¿cuáles de los programas le gustarían?

_____

3. Si te gustan los árboles y las plantas, ¿qué proyecto te gustaría hacer? ¿Y si te gustan los animales?

_____

_____

4. ¿Qué programas necesitarían médicos y enfermeros como voluntarios?

_____

5. ¿Qué programas tienen para gente que quiere aprender?

_____

_____

Conexión personal

If you were to begin a nonprofit organization, what would it do? What would you want to accomplish, and where? Write some notes about the organization you envision.

Nombre de la organización:

_____

¿Qué hace?

_____

¿Dónde lo hace?

_____

¿Cuáles son las metas (goals) de la organización?

_____

_____

_____

Para leer   *Dos profesiones únicas*

Reading Strategy

ANALYZE THE ACHIEVEMENTS Fill in the chart to understand each of the two men and their achievements.

Categorías	Iván Vallejo	Yucef Merhi
País		
Profesión		
¿Qué hizo?		
¿Por qué es una persona única?		

What You Need to Know

Known for its great past civilizations—the Incas, the Mayas, and the Aztecs—Latin America continues to make great contributions to world culture today. Great writers such as Gabriel García Márquez of Colombia and Isabel Allende of Chile have made their mark in literature. Singers and groups such as Gloria Estefan, Santana, and Shakira have crossed the line between the Spanish- and English-speaking worlds. In the world of sports, Latin America is home to gifted soccer players such as Alfredo Di Stefano of Argentina. In this reading, you will find out about two other Latin Americans who have pushed the boundaries of their chosen fields.

Dos profesiones únicas

Iván Vallejo es un **andinista** famoso de Ambato, Ecuador. Cuando tenía siete

5 años veía el volcán de Tungurahua desde su ciudad y soñaba con[1] **escalarlo.** Años después trabajaba durante

10 los veranos para comprarse su equipo[2] de andinismo. Empezó a escalar las montañas

Iván Vallejo

de la región. Comenzó con las más pequeñas

15 y terminó con la más alta de Ecuador: el Chimborazo.

Mientras tanto[3] seguía sus estudios. Estudió en la universidad para ser ingeniero químico[4]. Luego fue profesor de matemáticas

20 en la Politécnica de Quito y escalaba montañas en los veranos. Escaló varias montañas de los Andes, los Alpes y finalmente los Himalayas.

---

[1] **soñaba...** dreamed of   [2] gear
[3] **Mientras...** Meanwhile   [4] chemical

PALABRAS CLAVE
el (la) andinista *mountain climber*   **escalar** *to climb; to scale*

MÁRCALO GRAMÁTICA
Superlative adjectives are used to set apart one item from a group. They describe which items have the most or least of a certain quality. Look through the boxed text and circle the superlatives.

READER'S SUCCESS STRATEGY Before you read, look at the title, pictures, and captions and predict what the reading will be about.

A pensar...

Iván Vallejo is called both an **andinista** and an **alpinista.** Why do you think these two words are used to refer to mountain climbers? (**Activate Associated Knowledge, Infer**)

Do you feel comfortable
with Yucef Merhi's blend of
technology and poetry? Why
or why not? Do you think a
machine can create real poetry?
(Connect, Make Judgments)

Participantes en una exposición
interactiva de Yucef Merhi

Fue el primer
ecuatoriano que

25 alcanzó la **cima** del
Everest y uno de
pocos alpinistas
que lo hicieron sin
oxígeno suplementario, algo muy difícil de

30 **lograr:** solamente lo logra un seis por ciento
de las personas que lo **intentan**.

Yucef Merhi es artista, poeta y programador.
Es de Caracas, Venezuela. Cuando tenía ocho
años en 1985 empezó a experimentar con

35 la tecnología y el arte: le añadió un **teclado**
a su consola de videojuego Atari 2600 para
transformarla en computadora primitiva. Con
ella programó **películas** digitales.

Ahora sigue usando la tecnología

40 para crear[5] y presentar su arte y poesía. Usa
computadoras, videojuegos,
el Internet, telescopios
y muchas otras cosas
en sus exposiciones

45 internacionales. En
2005 **estrenó** su Super
Atari Poetry 2005, una
máquina interactiva. Las personas se sientan[6]
en frente de tres consolas de videojuego

---

[5] create   [6] **se...** sit

PALABRAS CLAVE

la cima *summit, peak*	**el teclado** *keyboard*
lograr *to achieve*	**la película** *movie, film*
intentar *to try; to attempt*	**estrenar** *to premier*

50 conectadas a tres televisores. Las consolas están programadas para crear poemas que **cambian** de colores. También inventó un Reloj Poético que transforma el tiempo en poesía y crea 86.400 poemas al día.

55 Merhi **no sólo** trabaja como artista-poeta-programador, **sino también** como consultor de informática[7] y diseñador de sitios Web para varias compañías.

---

[7] **consultor…** IT consultant

CHALLENGE If Yucef Merhi's Poetic Watch, or **Reloj Poético**, transforms time into poetry and creates 86,400 poems per day, how long does it take to create one poem? **(Infer)**

PALABRAS CLAVE
cambiar *to change*
no sólo… sino también *not only… but also*

Vocabulario de la lectura

Palabras clave

el (la) andinista *mountain climber*
cambiar *to change*
la cima *summit, peak*
escalar *to climb; to scale*
estrenar *to premier*
intentar *to try; to attempt*

lograr *to achieve*
no sólo… sino también *not only … but also*
la película *movie, film*
el teclado *keyboard*

A. Escoge el antónimo para cada **Palabra clave.** Escribe la letra de la respuesta en el espacio en blanco.

_____ **1.** cambiar

_____ **2.** escalar

_____ **3.** estrenar

_____ **4.** intentar

_____ **5.** lograr

a. quedarse igual; ser algo siempre lo mismo

b. no hacer nada

c. bajar

d. no alcanzar *(reach)* un objetivo

e. hacer algo por última vez

B. Contesta cada pregunta escribiendo una de las **Palabras clave** en el espacio en blanco.

1. ¿Cuál es otra palabra para un alpinista? _____

2. ¿Con qué escribes en una computadora? _____

3. Con una cámara fotográfica, puedes tomar fotografías. ¿Qué puedes tomar

con una cámara de video? _____

4. Si escalas una montaña, ¿adónde llegas? _____

5. ¿Qué puedes decir para mostrar que eres estudiante y también artista?

_____

¿Comprendiste?

1. ¿Cuándo empezó Iván Vallejo a pensar en escalar montañas?

_____

2. ¿Qué lo hace un alpinista—o andinista—especial?

_____

3. ¿Quién es Yucef Merhi? ¿Cuál es su profesión?

_____

_____

4. ¿Qué hizo cuando tenía ocho años? ¿Y qué hace ahora?

_____

_____

Conexión personal

What is your dream job? And what would it take to be at the top of that profession? In the word web below, write the profession of your dreams. It does not have to be an existing field; you can invent one. In the outer circles, write what you would have to do to make it to the top of your chosen profession.

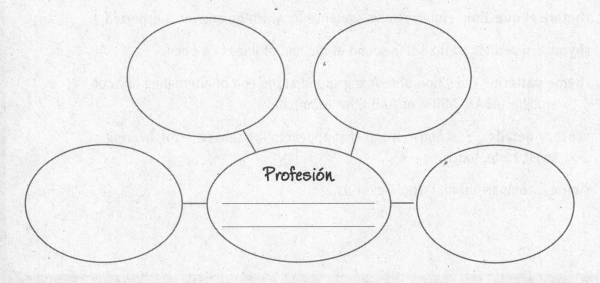

Profesión

_____

_____

Literary terms

alliteration   repetition of the same sounds in a phrase or a line of poetry

Anglicism   use of English words in another language

antithesis   contrast between a word or a phrase and another that means the opposite

catalog   list of people, things, or attributes in a narration or poem

character   person in a literary work

flashback   scene from the past that interrupts the ongoing action of a work

hyperbole   exaggerated description of a person or thing

irony   contrast between what is stated and what is meant or between what is expected and what actually happens

metaphor   direct comparison between two unlike things

onomatopoeia   use of words to imitate the sound of something

parallelism   related ideas phrased in similar ways

personification   use of human characteristics to describe an animal or an object

protagonist   main character of a work

repetition   recurring sounds, words, or phrases to give emphasis

rhetorical question   interrogative sentence to which no answer is expected

rhyme   repetition of the same sound at the end of lines in a poem

rhyme pattern   repetition of rhyming sound at the end of alternating lines of a poem (ABAB, ABBA, or AABB, for example)

sensory details   descriptive words that appeal to the senses (sight, hearing, smell, taste, touch)

simile   comparison that uses *like* or *as*

Literatura adicional

In this section you will find literary readings in Spanish that range from poems to excerpts from novels, short stories, and other works. Each reading has biographical information about the author and background information about the selection. Like the *Lecturas culturales* readings, the literary readings have reading strategies, reading tips, reader's success strategies, critical-thinking questions, vocabulary activities, comprehension questions, and a short writing activity to help you understand each selection. There is also a **Márcalo** feature for literary analysis of the readings.

Para leer   *Senderos fronterizos*

Reading Strategy

CONNECT TO YOUR OWN LIFE When you read, you can connect
story events or a character's actions to your own life. As you read
this excerpt from *Senderos fronterizos*, try to think of similar
experiences you have had in your own life. Use the chart to connect
the setting, the events, and what Francisco Jiménez says and does
to your experiences.

Lo que Francisco y yo tenemos en común	En qué somos diferentes Francisco y yo
Tenemos que escribir informes de lectura	

What You Need to Know

This reading is from the book *Senderos fronterizos* (2002) by Francisco
Jiménez, originally published in English as *Breaking Through* in 2001.
It is a continuation of *Cajas de cartón (The Circuit)*. Each book is an
autobiography, the story of a person's life written by that person. In this
excerpt, Francisco Jiménez is in his second year of high school. He has
handed in a corrected assignment, in which he has written about his
personal experience of being a migrant worker. His English teacher gives
him a copy of *The Grapes of Wrath* (1939) to read. This novel by John
Steinbeck tells the story of the Joads, a poor farm family that migrates
from Oklahoma to California in search of a better life during the Great
Depression. Francisco Jiménez makes connections between the novel and
his own life.

Sobre el autor

Francisco Jiménez (1943–) inmigró con su familia a California desde Tlaquepaque, México, cuando tenía cuatro años. Siendo un niño, trabajó en los campos de California y su libro autobiográfico *Cajas de cartón* narra la historia de esos años. *Senderos fronterizos* habla de sus experiencias en la escuela secundaria. Se graduó de la Universidad de Santa Clara. Recibió su maestría y su doctorado en la Universidad de Columbia en Nueva York. Actualmente enseña lenguas y literatura en la Universidad de Santa Clara, donde es director del programa de estudios étnicos. Vive en Santa Clara, California, con su esposa y sus tres hijos.

Senderos fronterizos

Al día siguiente, después de la clase, le **entregué** a la señorita Bell mi trabajo reelaborado. Ella lo miró rápidamente, lo colocó[1] sobre una pila de papeles encima de

5 su escritorio y tomó en sus manos un libro.

—¿Has leído alguna vez *The Grapes of Wrath*? —me preguntó—. Es una maravillosa novela de John Steinbeck.

—No —dije yo, preguntándome qué
10 significaba la palabra *wrath*.

---

[1] placed

PALABRAS CLAVE
   entregar *to turn in; to hand over*

READING TIP Note that italics are used to indicate the book title *The Grapes of Wrath* as well as English words *(locker, grapes, wrath, Tent City)* within the Spanish text.

APUNTES

CHALLENGE Have you ever read *The Grapes of Wrath*? If so, what did you think of it? If not, would you like to read it? Why or why not? **(Connect)**

APUNTES

APUNTES

_____

_____

_____

_____

_____

_____

_____

_____

_____

_____

—Quisiera que la leyeras[2] —dijo ella, y me la entregó—. Creo que la vas a disfrutar. Puedes leerla para tu informe de lectura[3].

15 «¿De dónde voy a sacar tiempo para leer un libro tan **grueso**?» pensé yo, pasando mis dedos sobre el **lomo** grueso del libro. Yo tenía planeado leer un libro más pequeño para mi informe de lectura. La señorita Bell debió haber notado el dolor[4] en mi rostro[5], porque
20 agregó[6]: —Tú recibirás créditos extra, por ser un libro **extenso**—. Entonces me sentí mejor.

—¡Gracias! —dije—. Eso me dará una oportunidad de mejorar mis **calificaciones**. Su amable sonrisa me hacía pensar en Mamá
25 y en la bendición[7] que ella nos daba cada mañana cuando yo salía de casa.

Después de mi última clase saqué de mi _locker_ los libros y carpetas[8] que necesitaba y me dirigí[9] caminando a la biblioteca pública
30 para estudiar antes de irme a trabajar a las cinco. Revisé bien para asegurarme de que llevaba conmigo la novela. En el camino, iba pensando en cómo podría arreglármelas para leer un libro tan largo. Sentía su peso[10] en

---

[2] **Quisiera…** I would like you to read it
[3] **informe…** book report   [4] distress   [5] face   [6] added
[7] blessing   [8] folders   [9] I went   [10] weight

PALABRAS CLAVE
grueso(a) _thick_	**extenso(a)** _long, extensive_
el lomo _spine_	**la calificación** _grade, mark_

35 los hombros y la nuca[11]. Apuré[12] mis pasos,
    adelantando[13] a otros estudiantes a derecha y
    a izquierda. A lo lejos se oían los pitazos[14] de
    los estudiantes que circulaban[15] en sus carros,
    haciendo sonar el claxon[16]. Me apuré a llegar a
40 la biblioteca y me fui directamente a mi mesa
    en la esquina posterior izquierda, apartada de
    la recepción. Apilé mis libros y mis carpetas
    encima de la mesa.

    Respiré[17] profundamente, tomé la novela y la
45 puse frente a mí. Tomé de la pila mi gastado[18]
    diccionario de bolsillo[19] y lo puse a un lado.
    Susurré[20] el título: *The Grapes of Wrath*. La
    palabra *grapes* me recordaba haber trabajado
    en los **viñedos** del señor Sullivan en Fresno.
50 Busqué la palabra *wrath* y pensé en la **cólera**
    que sentí cuando perdí mi libretita azul,
    durante un incendio[21] en Orosí. Empecé a leer.
    Era difícil. Tenía que buscar en el diccionario el
    significado de muchas palabras pero, aún así,
55 seguí leyendo. Quería saber más acerca de la
    familia Joad, que había tenido que abandonar
    su **hogar** en Oklahoma para buscar trabajo y
    una vida mejor en California. Se me pasó el
    tiempo. Sin darme cuenta, habían pasado las
60 cinco. Llegué tarde al trabajo.

---

[11] nape of the neck	[12] I hurried	[13] passing
[14] toots of a car horn	[15] were driving (along)	
[16] **haciendo...** honking the horn		
[17] I breathed	[18] worn out	[19] pocket
[20] I whispered	[21] fire	

PALABRAS CLAVE

el viñedo *vineyard*   el hogar *home*
la cólera *anger, fury*

CHALLENGE What did the word *grapes* in the title of the novel remind Francisco of? Circle the correct answer. **(Clarify)**

buying grapes at the supermarket

selling grapes at a produce stand

eating grapes at a picnic

picking grapes at a vineyard

APUNTES

CHALLENGE Read the boxed text. What do you think Francisco Jiménez means? (Analyze)

APUNTES

Cuando llegué a casa esa noche, continué leyendo hasta la una de la madrugada[22]. Esa noche **soñé** que mi familia estaba empacando nuestras cosas a fin de **mudarnos** a Fresno
65 para **pizcar** uvas. «¡Ya no tenemos que mudarnos más! ¡Tengo que ir a la escuela!», gritaba yo repetidamente, pero Papá y Mamá no podían oírme. Me desperté **agotado.**

La noche del sábado, no quise ir al baile de la
70 escuela y me quedé en casa leyendo la novela. Seguía batallando con la lectura, pero no podía abandonarla. Finalmente entendí lo que la señorita Bell me quiso dar a entender cuando me dijo que leyera por placer[23]. Yo
75 podía identificarme con lo que estaba leyendo. La familia Joad era pobre y viajaba de un lugar a otro en una carcacha[24], buscando trabajo. Ellos pizcaban uvas y algodón[25], y vivían en campamentos de trabajadores
80 similares a aquellos en que nosotros habíamos vivido, como *Tent City*, en Santa María. Ma Joad era como Mamá y Pa Joad tenía **parecido** a Papá. Aunque ellos no fueran mexicanos y hablaran sólo inglés, tenían
85 muchas experiencias en común con mi familia. Yo me sentía afectado por las cosas que les

[22] **de...** in the morning
[23] **leyera...** to read for pleasure   [24] jalopy
[25] cotton

PALABRAS CLAVE

soñar *to dream*		**agotado(a)** *exhausted*
mudarse *to move*		**el parecido** *similarity, resemblance*
pizcar *to pick*		

sucedían. Me enojaba con los granjeros[26] que los maltrataban[27] y me alegraba cuando Tom Joad protestaba y peleaba por sus

90 derechos[28]. Él me recordaba a mi amigo don Gabriel, el bracero[29] que se enfrentó[30] a Díaz, el contratista de jornaleros[31], quien intentó obligar a don Gabriel a jalar el arado[32] como si fuera un buey[33].

95 Después de haber terminado la lectura de la novela, yo no podía sacármela de la **mente.** Pasé pensando en ella muchos días, aún después de haberle presentado mi informe de lectura a la señorita Bell. A ella debió haberle

100 gustado lo que escribí, porque me dio una buena nota. Mi éxito me alegró pero, esta vez, la nota me pareció menos importante que lo que yo había aprendido leyendo el libro.

---

[26] farmers   [27] mistreated
[28] **peleaba...** fought for his rights
[29] Mexican migrant worker (from the word *brazo*)
[30] confronted   [31] contractor of day laborers
[32] **jalar...** to pull the plow
[33] ox

MÁRCALO ANÁLISIS A simile is a comparison of one thing to another using the word **como** in Spanish or the words *like* or *as* in English: for example, *as tall as a tree*. Find and circle the simile on this page.

APUNTES

A pensar...

1. How are the Joads like Francisco's family? How are they different? (**Compare and Contrast**)

2. Why do you think Francisco's teacher gave him *The Grapes of Wrath* to read? (**Infer**)

PALABRAS CLAVE
suceder *to happen*   **la mente** *mind*

Vocabulario de la lectura

Palabras clave

agotado(a) *exhausted*

la calificación *grade, mark*

la cólera *anger, fury*

entregar *to turn in; to hand over*

extenso(a) *long, extensive*

grueso(a) *thick*

el hogar *home*

el lomo *spine*

la mente *mind*

mudarse *to move*

el parecido *similarity, resemblance*

pizcar *to pick*

soñar *to dream*

suceder *to happen*

el viñedo *vineyard*

A. Al lado de cada par de palabras, escribe si las palabras son sinónimos o antónimos. Los sinónimos son palabras con el mismo significado o un significado similar. Los antónimos son palabras con significados opuestos.

1. cansado — agotado _____

2. permanecer — mudarse _____

3. pasar — suceder _____

4. delgado — grueso _____

5. diferencia — parecido _____

B. Escribe un párrafo corto sobre un informe de lectura. Puede ser un informe por ti o un informe imaginario. Usa por lo menos cuatro de las **Palabras clave.**

_____

_____

_____

_____

_____

_____

_____

_____

¿Comprendiste?

1. ¿Cómo se llama la maestra de inglés de Francisco?

_____

2. ¿Qué es *The Grapes of Wrath*?

_____

3. ¿Por qué tiene Francisco que leer *The Grapes of Wrath*?

_____

4. ¿Cómo es la lectura de la novela para Francisco?

_____

_____

5. ¿A la maestra le gusta el informe de lectura de Francisco? ¿Cómo lo sabes?

_____

Conexión personal

The Grapes of Wrath lingers in
the mind of Francisco Jiménez.
Is there a book that has made
a similar impression on you?
Describe the book. Why did it
interest you so much? Write about
the book in the notebook at the
right.

Un gran libro

_____

_____

_____

_____

_____

_____

_____

_____

Para leer   *Escrituras*

Reading Strategy

IDENTIFY THE AUTHOR'S PURPOSE The reason for creating a particular literary work is the author's purpose. A writer may write to entertain, to inform, to express an opinion, or to persuade readers to do or believe something. A particular text may have only one purpose, while others may have two or more. As you read the three pieces by Frida Kahlo, place one or more check marks in the chart below to show the purpose or purposes of each.

Obra	Propósito de la autora			
	Entretener	Informar	Expresar una opinión	Persuadir
Declaración				
Retrato de Diego				
Invitación				

What You Need to Know

This reading is three pieces of prose and poetry by Mexican artist Frida Kahlo (1907–1954). The first is a declaration requested by the Instituto Nacional de Bellas Artes (INBA). The statement was displayed next to a painting by Kahlo in a 1947 exhibit of self-portraits by Mexican artists at the Palacio de Bellas Artes in Mexico City. The second is the last paragraph of **«Retrato de Diego»** about her husband. It was written especially for the catalog to the exhibit *Diego Rivera, cincuenta años de labor artística* at the Palacio de Bellas Artes in 1949. The last is an invitation to Kahlo's only solo exhibition in Mexico, which took place in 1953 at the Galería de Arte Contemporáneo directed by Lola Álvarez Bravo.

Sobre la autora

Frida Kahlo nació en el barrio de Coyoacán de la Ciudad de México en 1907. En 1926, tuvo un terrible accidente en el que se fracturó la columna vertebral, la pelvis, la clavícula, tres costillas, la pierna y el pie derecho. Su arte refleja el dolor que sufrió continuamente el resto de su vida como resultado del accidente. Se sometió a más de treinta operaciones durante su vida. Se casó con el pintor Diego Rivera en 1929. (Se divorciaron pero volvieron a casarse.) Murió en 1954 en su casa de Coyoacán, que hoy es un museo. Según Kahlo, «pensaron que yo era surrealista, pero no lo fui. Nunca pinté mis sueños, sólo pinté mi propia realidad».

Declaración solicitada por el INBA

Comencé a pintar... por puro aburrimiento de estar **encamada** durante un año, después de sufrir un accidente en el que me fracturé la espina dorsal, un pie y otros huesos[1]. Tenía
5 entonces dieciséis años y mucho entusiasmo por estudiar la carrera de medicina. Pero todo lo frustró[2] el choque[3] entre un camión[4] de Coyoacán y un tranvía[5] de Tlalpan... Como era joven, esta desgracia[6] no tomó entonces
10 **rasgos** trágicos: sentía energía suficiente para hacer cualquier[7] cosa en lugar de estudiar para médico. Y sin darme mucha cuenta comencé a pintar.

---

[1] bones   [2] thwarted   [3] collision
[4] Mexican word for *bus*   [5] trolley, streetcar
[6] mishap, misfortune   [7] any

PALABRAS CLAVE
   encamado(a)   *bedridden*   **el rasgo**   *trait, characteristic*

READING TIP Remember the art vocabulary that you previously learned: **pintar, pintura, retrato, exposición, galería.**

APUNTES

_____

_____

_____

_____

_____

A pensar...

1. Why did Frida Kahlo begin to paint? (**Summarize**)

_____

_____

_____

_____

2. What does this statement reveal to you about Frida Kahlo's spirit? (**Draw Conclusions**)

_____

_____

_____

_____

_____

READER'S SUCCESS STRATEGY Use words you already know to help you figure out new words that are part of the same word family. For example, you know the adjective **aburrido(a)** and the verb **aburrirse**. What do you think the noun **aburrimiento** in line 1 means? You also know the verb **conocer**. What do you think the noun **conocimiento** in line 26 means? Write your answers below.

_____

_____

_____

CHALLENGE Surrealism was a 20th-century artistic movement. It attempted to express the workings of the subconscious and was characterized by fantastic imagery. Do you think that the painting on this page is surrealistic, the expression of Frida Kahlo's own reality (as she referred to her art), or perhaps both? **(Draw Conclusions)**

_____

_____

_____

_____

_____

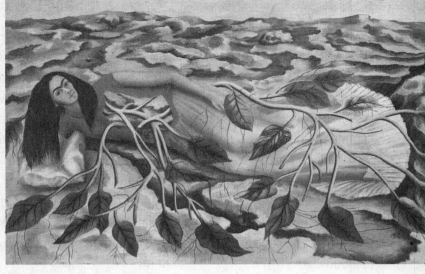

Raíces, *1943*

Realmente no sé si mis pinturas son o no

15 surrealistas, pero sí sé que son la más franca expresión de mí misma, sin tomar jamás en consideración ni juicios[8] ni prejuicios[9] de nadie. He pintado poco, sin el menor deseo de gloria ni ambición, con la convicción de,

20 antes que todo, darme gusto, y después poder ganarme la vida con mi **oficio.** De los viajes que hice, viendo y observando todo lo que pude, magnífica pintura y muy mala también, saqué dos cosas positivas: tratar hasta donde

25 pueda de ser siempre yo misma, y el amargo[10] conocimiento de que muchas vidas no serían suficientes para pintar como yo quisiera y todo lo que quisiera.

---

[8] opinions, judgments   [9] prejudices, biases   [10] bitter, painful

PALABRAS CLAVE
   el oficio   *work; craft*

Retrato de Diego

Ningunas palabras describirán la inmensa
ternura de Diego por las cosas que tienen
belleza; su **cariño** por los seres que no tienen
que ver en la presente sociedad de clases; o
5 su respeto por los que están oprimidos[11] por
la misma. Tiene especial adoración por los
indios a quienes lo liga[12] su sangre; los quiere
entrañablemente[13] por su elegancia, por su
belleza y por ser la flor viva de la tradición
10 cultural de América. Quiere a los niños, a
todos los animales, con predilección a los
perros pelones[14] mexicanos y a los pájaros,
a las plantas y a las piedras. Ama a todos
los seres sin ser dócil ni neutral. Es muy
15 cariñoso pero nunca **se entrega;** por esto, y
porque apenas tiene tiempo para dedicarse a
las relaciones personales, le llaman ingrato.
Es respetuoso[15] y fino[16] y nada le violenta[17]
más que la falta de respeto de los demás y el
20 abuso. No soporta el truco o el engaño
solapado[18]; lo que en México se llama
«tomadura de pelo[19]». Prefiere tener enemigos
inteligentes que aliados estúpidos. De
temperamento es más bien alegre, pero le
25 irrita enormemente que le quiten el tiempo en
el trabajo. Su diversión es el trabajo mismo;

---

[11] oppressed   [12] links   [13] deeply, dearly
[14] hairless   [15] respectful   [16] well-mannered
[17] infuriates, outrages
[18] **engaño...** underhanded trick or deception
[19] **tomadura...** practical joke, hoax

PALABRAS CLAVE

la ternura *tenderness*	**entregarse** *to surrender*
el cariño *affection*	

MÁRCALO ▷ **ANÁLISIS** A metaphor is the direct comparison of two unlike things, such as *All the world's a stage*. Find and circle the metaphor on this page.

APUNTES

CHALLENGE Read the boxed text. What do you think Kahlo means to say about her husband Diego Rivera? (Analyze)

APUNTES

Frida y Diego, *1931*

odia[20] las reuniones sociales y le maravillan las fiestas verdaderamente populares.

A veces es tímido, y así como le fascina

30 conversar y discutir con todos, le encanta a veces estar absolutamente solo. Nunca se aburre porque todo le interesa; estudiando, analizando y profundizando en[21] todas las manifestaciones de la vida. No es sentimental

35 pero sí intensamente emotivo[22] y apasionado. Le desespera[23] la inercia porque él es una corriente continua, viva y potente[24]. De buen gusto extraordinario, admira y aprecia todo lo que contiene belleza, lo mismo si vibra en

---

[20] hates, loathes   [21] **profundizando...** delving into
[22] emotional   [23] exasperates   [24] powerful

⫿⫿ MÁRCALO ⟩ ANÁLISIS

Remember that a simile is a comparison using the word **como** (like, as). Find and circle the simile on this page. On the lines below, write some of the similarities Kahlo describes.

40 una mujer o en una montaña. Perfectamente
equilibrado[25] en todas sus emociones, sus
sensaciones y sus hechos[26], a los que mueve
la dialéctica materialista, precisa y real, nunca
se entrega. Como los cactus de su tierra, crece
45 fuerte y **asombroso,** lo mismo en la arena que
en la piedra; florece[27] con el rojo más vivo, el
blanco más transparente y el amarillo solar;
revestido de[28] espinas, resguarda[29] dentro su
ternura; vive con su savia[30] fuerte dentro de
50 un medio feroz; ilumina solitario como sol
vengador[31] del gris de la piedra; sus raíces[32]
viven a pesar de que lo arranquen[33] de la
tierra, sobrepasando la angustia de la **soledad**
y de la tristeza y de todas las debilidades[34]
55 que a otros seres doblegan[35]. Se levanta con
sorprendente **fuerza** y, como ninguna otra
planta, florece y da frutos.

---

[25] stable, balanced   [26] actions   [27] flowers, blooms; flourishes
[28] **revestido...** covered with   [29] protected
[30] sap; vigor, energy   [31] avenging   [32] roots
[33] **a pesar...** despite being pulled out   [34] weaknesses
[35] bend, force to yield or give in

APUNTES

PALABRAS CLAVE

la sensación *feeling*   **la soledad** *solitude*
asombroso(a) *amazing, astonishing*   **la fuerza** *strength; force*

READING TIP Note the use of a contraction for **de esta** at the end of the second stanza of the poem.

███ MÁRCALO ⟩ ANÁLISIS
Rhyme is the repetition of sounds at the ends of words. Find and circle words at the ends of lines of the poem that rhyme. What pattern do you notice? Write it below.

_____

_____

_____

A pensar...

1. Why do you think Kahlo wrote this invitation as a poem? (**Make Judgments**)

_____

_____

_____

_____

2. If you had received this invitation, would you have gone to see Kahlo's exhibit? Why or why not? (**Connect**)

_____

_____

_____

_____

_____

_____

Invitación de Frida Kahlo

para su exposición individual en
la Galería de Arte Contemporáneo,
inaugurada el 13 de abril de 1953

Con amistad y cariño
nacido del corazón
tengo el gusto de invitarte
a mi humilde[36] exposición.

5   A las ocho de la noche
—pues reloj tienes al cabo[37]—
te espero en la Galería
d'esta Lola Álvarez Bravo.

Se encuentra en Amberes 12
10 y con puertas a la calle,
de suerte que no te pierdes
porque se acaba el detalle.

_____
[36] humble, modest
[37] **al...** after all

CHALLENGE After reading all three pieces and looking at the paintings, how would you describe Frida Kahlo? **(Make Judgments)**

Sólo quiero que me digas
tu opinión buena y sincera.
15 Eres leído y escribido[38];
tu saber es de primera [39].

Estos cuadros de pintura
pinté con mis propias manos
y esperan en las paredes
20 que gusten a mis hermanos

Bueno, mi cuate[40] querido:
con amistad verdadera
te lo agradece[41] en el **alma**
Frida Kahlo de Rivera.

Coyoacán – 1953

---

[38] colloquial expression for *learned*
[39] first-rate, excellent
[40] Mexican word for *buddy*
[41] is grateful, thanks

APUNTES

PALABRAS CLAVE
el alma (fem.)   *soul, spirit*

Vocabulario de la lectura

Palabras clave

el alma (fem.) *soul, spirit*	**el oficio** *work; craft*
asombroso(a) *amazing, astonishing*	**el rasgo** *trait, characteristic*
el cariño *affection*	**la sensación** *feeling*
encamado(a) *bedridden*	**la soledad** *solitude*
entregarse *to surrender*	**la ternura** *tenderness*
la fuerza *strength; force*	

A. Para cada palabra de la primera columna, busca la definición en la segunda columna. Escribe la letra de la definición correcta en el espacio en blanco.

_____ 1. rasgo   A. energía, vitalidad

_____ 2. cariño   B. amor, devoción

_____ 3. oficio   C. espíritu, esencia

_____ 4. fuerza   D. cualidad

_____ 5. alma   E. trabajo, empleo

B. Escribe una descripción corta de Frida Kahlo. Usa por lo menos tres de las **Palabras clave.**

_____

_____

_____

_____

_____

_____

_____

_____

¿Comprendiste?

1. ¿Qué quería estudiar Frida Kahlo?

_____

2. ¿Qué accidente sufrió?

_____

3. ¿Con qué planta comparó a su esposo Diego Rivera?

_____

4. ¿Qué información sobre la exposición da la invitación?

_____

Conexión personal

Imagine that you are an art reviewer. What do you think of Frida Kahlo's paintings? Write your opinion of the Kahlo paintings that appear on these pages. Use the notebook at the right.

Las pinturas de Frida Kahlo

_____

_____

_____

_____

_____

_____

_____

_____

_____

LITERATURA ADICIONAL

Para leer   *A Julia de Burgos*

Reading Strategy

CLARIFY THE MEANING OF A POEM The process of stopping while reading to quickly review what has happened and to look for answers to questions you may have is called clarifying.
Complete the chart below by doing the following:

- Divide the poem into six sections (the length of the sections may vary).
- Read the first section.
- Stop to clarify that section.
- Paraphrase what that section is about in one of the boxes.
- Continue to read and clarify the other five sections of the poem in the same manner.

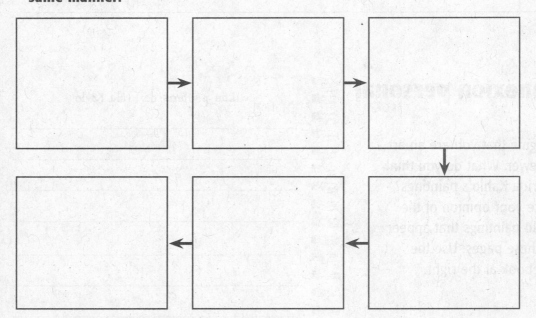

What You Need to Know

This reading is the poem **«A Julia de Burgos»** by the Puerto Rican poet Julia de Burgos (1914–1953). In this poem Julia de Burgos talks with herself. Julia, the poet, addresses Julia, the society woman. Julia de Burgos explores the contradictions within herself, between her inner being and her outer shell. She also comments on the status of women in Puerto Rico.

Sobre la autora

Julia de Burgos nació en Carolina (Bayamón), Puerto Rico, en 1914, siendo la mayor de trece hermanos. Escritora y poeta, es casi una leyenda en Puerto Rico. Después de vivir en zonas provincianas de Puerto Rico, se mudó a Cuba y luego a Nueva York. Publicó sólo dos libros durante su vida: *Poemas en 20 surcos* (1938) y *Canción de la verdad sencilla* (1939). Murió en Nueva York en 1953. Su libro *El mar y tú* se publicó un año después de su muerte.

A Julia de Burgos

Ya las gentes murmuran que yo soy tu
    enemiga
porque dicen que en verso doy al mundo
    tu yo.

5 **Mienten,** Julia de Burgos. Mienten,
    Julia de Burgos.

> La que se alza[1] en mis versos no es tu voz:
>   es mi voz
> porque tú eres **ropaje** y la esencia soy yo;
> 10 y el más profundo abismo se tiende[2] entre
>   las dos.

Tú eres fría muñeca de mentira social,
y yo, viril destello[3] de la humana verdad.

Tú, **miel** de cortesanas[4] hipocresías; yo no;
15 que en todos mis poemas desnudo[5] el corazón.

---

[1] rises   [2] stretches out, spreads   [3] flash, glimmer   [4] courtly
[5] I lay bare

PALABRAS CLAVE
mentir *to lie*   **la miel** *honey*
el ropaje *vestment*

READING TIP Poems often contain repeated elements and patterns. Look for repetition and patterns as you read the poem. Note that the indented words are part of the previous line.

APUNTES

CHALLENGE Read the boxed text. What do you think Julia de Burgos means? **(Analyze)**

MÁRCALO ANÁLISIS
Antithesis is the contrast of a word, phrase, or idea against another with the opposite meaning. **Mentira** and **verdad** are an example. Find and circle other uses of antithesis in the poem. Write the pairs of words on the lines below.

READER'S SUCCESS STRATEGY Read the poem aloud. Pause at the commas, colons, and semicolons and stop at the periods, rather than stopping at the end of each line. This will help you understand the poet's thoughts.

APUNTES

Tú eres como tu mundo, egoísta; yo no;
que en todo me lo juego[6] a ser lo que soy yo.

Tú eres sólo la grave señora señorona[7];
yo no; yo soy la vida, la fuerza, la mujer.

20 Tú eres de tu **marido,** de tu **amo;** yo no;
yo de nadie, o de todos, porque a todos,
                              a todos,
en mi limpio sentir y en mi pensar me doy.

Tú te rizas[8] el pelo y te pintas; yo no;
25 a mí me riza el viento; a mí me pinta el sol.

Tú eres dama casera[9], resignada, **sumisa,**
atada[10] a los prejuicios de los hombres; yo no;
que yo soy Rocinante[11] corriendo **desbocado**
olfateando[12] horizontes de justicia de Dios.

30 Tú en ti misma no **mandas;** a ti todos te
                              mandan;
en ti mandan tu esposo, tus padres, tus
                              parientes,
el cura[13], la modista[14], el teatro, el casino[15],
35 el auto, las alhajas[16], el banquete, el champán,
el cielo[17] y el infierno, y el qué dirán[18] social.

---

[6] **me...** I risk   [7] great lady   [8] **Tú...** You curl
[9] homebody   [10] tied
[11] the name Don Quixote gave his horse
[12] smelling, scenting out   [13] priest   [14] dressmaker
[15] social club   [16] jewels, treasures   [17] heaven
[18] what people will say

PALABRAS CLAVE

el marido *husband*	**desbocado(a)** *runaway*
el amo *master*	**mandar** *to be in command or charge*
sumiso(a) *submissive*	

En mí no, que en mí manda mi solo corazón,
mi solo pensamiento; quien manda en mí
       soy yo.
40 Tú, flor de aristocracia; y yo, la flor del pueblo[19].
Tú en ti lo tienes todo y a todos se lo debes,
mientras que yo, mi nada a nadie se la debo.

Tú, clavada[20] al estático dividendo ancestral,
y yo, un uno en la cifra[21] del divisor social,
45 somos el duelo a muerte que **se acerca** fatal.

Cuando las multitudes corran alborotadas[22]
dejando atrás cenizas de injusticias quemadas,
y cuando con la **tea** de las siete virtudes,
tras los siete pecados[23], corran las multitudes,
50 contra ti, y contra todo lo injusto y
       lo inhumano,
yo iré en medio de ellas con la tea en la mano.

---

[19] (common) people   [20] nailed, stuck   [21] number
[22] riotous, rowdy   [23] sins

PALABRAS CLAVE
acercarse *to approach*   la tea *torch*

A pensar...

1. What word begins many stanzas of the poem? How is the use of this word helpful in establishing a conversation? **(Evaluate)**

_____

_____

_____

_____

2. Why do you think the poet gave the poem the title she did? **(Draw Conclusions)**

_____

_____

_____

_____

_____

APUNTES

_____

_____

_____

_____

_____

_____

Vocabulario de la lectura

Palabras clave

acercarse *to approach*	**el marido** *husband*	**el ropaje** *vestment*
el amo *master*	**mentir** *to lie*	**sumiso(a)** *submissive*
desbocado(a) *runaway*	**la miel** *honey*	**la tea** *torch*
mandar *to be in command or charge*		

A. En el espacio en blanco que aparece al lado de cada grupo de frases, escribe la **Palabra clave** que corresponda con cada serie de pistas.

1. descontrolado, caballo _____

2. dulce, comer _____

3. patrón, jefe, dueño; mandar _____

4. luz, llevar, la Estatua de la Libertad _____

5. dócil, obediente, subordinado _____

B. Completa cada analogía con una de las **Palabras clave.** En una analogía, las últimas dos palabras deben estar relacionadas del mismo modo que las primeras dos palabras.

1. COMPRENDER : ENTENDER : : falsear : _____

2. DAR : RECIBIR : : irse : _____

3. MESERO : CAMARERO : : esposo : _____

4. INTERIOR : ESENCIA : : exterior : _____

5. VENDER : COMPRAR : : seguir : _____

¿Comprendiste?

1. ¿Quién es «yo» en el poema? ¿Quién es «tú»?

_____

_____

2. ¿Qué son las dos juntas?

_____

_____

3. ¿Cómo es la dama casera en el poema?

_____

_____

4. ¿Qué va a llevar la poeta en la mano al final?

_____

_____

Conexión personal

Imagine that you are writing a poem about yourself. Make a list of Spanish words and phrases you would use to describe yourself. You may even use antithesis, as Julia de Burgos does in her poem. Write your list of descriptive words in the notebook at the right.

Yo

_____

_____

_____

_____

_____

_____

_____

_____

_____

_____

Para leer   *Platero y yo*

Reading Strategy

ANALYZE WORD CHOICE Writers choose their words with care in order to express their thoughts and feelings accurately. Through careful word choice, a writer can make readers feel a certain way or help readers visualize a scene. As you read *Platero y yo*, think about how certain words affect you as a reader. Use the chart below to record interesting words and phrases and the ideas or feelings they convey.

Palabras y frases	Lo que expresan
cascabeleo ideal	parece música

What You Need to Know

This reading is three chapters of *Platero y yo*, a prose poem by the Spanish writer Juan Ramón Jiménez (1881–1958). It was first published in 1914 with 64 chapters chosen by the publisher. The first complete edition was published in 1917 with the original 136 chapters plus two later ones. The subtitle of the book is *Elegía andaluza*. The book is Jiménez's impressions and memories of his hometown Moguer in Andalusia, but it is not a diary or an autobiography. The Platero of the title is a silver-colored donkey, a synthesis of all the donkeys the poet had as a boy. Donkeys were very common in rural areas like Moguer because they could be used to carry small loads and they needed less care than a horse or a mule.

READING TIP Imagine, or visualize, what Juan Ramón Jiménez describes in *Platero y yo*. Don't let the words you don't know slow you down. Try to focus on the strongest images.

APUNTES

Sobre el autor

Juan Ramón Jiménez es uno de los poetas españoles más reconocidos del siglo XX. Nació en Moguer, en la provincia andaluza de Huelva en 1881. Su infancia en Moguer lo inspiraría a escribir *Platero y yo*. Sus libros de poesía incluyen *Arias tristes* (1903), *Laberinto* (1913) y *Diario de un poeta recién casado* (1916). *Españoles de tres mundos* (1942) es un ejemplo de su prosa. En 1936 abandonó España a causa de la Guerra Civil española y vivió por años en Cuba, Estados Unidos y Puerto Rico. Murió en San Juan, Puerto Rico, en 1958, dos años después de recibir el premio Nobel de literatura.

Platero y yo

Platero

Platero es pequeño, peludo[1], **suave;** tan **blando** por fuera, que se diría todo de algodón, que no lleva huesos. Sólo los espejos de azabache[2] de sus ojos son duros cual dos
5 escarabajos[3] de cristal negro.

Lo dejo **suelto,** y se va al prado[4], y acaricia tibiamente[5] con su **hocico,** rozándolas[6] apenas, las florecillas rosas, celestes[7] y gualdas[8]... Lo llamo dulcemente: «¿Platero?», y
10 viene a mí con un trotecillo alegre que parece que se ríe, en no sé qué cascabeleo[9] ideal...

---

[1] shaggy	[2] jet black	[3] scarabs, a type of black beetle
[4] meadow, field	[5] indifferently
[6] brushing or rubbing against	[7] sky blue
[8] yellow	[9] sound of bells

MÁRCALO **ANÁLISIS**
Personification is the attribution of human characteristics to an object, animal, or idea. Juan Ramón Jiménez describes Platero in a way that makes the donkey seem like a person. Find and circle examples of the personification of Platero in this chapter.

APUNTES

PALABRAS CLAVE
suave *soft, smooth; delicate*
blando(a) *soft*
suelto(a) *loose, untied*
el hocico *muzzle, snout*

_____

_____

_____

A pensar...

1. Read the boxed text. What do you think that Juan Ramón Jiménez means to say about Platero? **(Analyze)**

_____

_____

_____

2. What do you think the men mean when they say that Platero «**tiene acero**»? **(Infer)**

_____

_____

Come cuanto le doy. Le gustan las naranjas[10], mandarinas, las uvas moscateles, todas de ámbar, los higos[11] morados, con su cristalina

15 gotita de miel...

Es **tierno** y mimoso[12] igual que[13] un niño, que una niña...; pero fuerte y seco por dentro, como de piedra. Cuando paso sobre él, los domingos, por las últimas callejas[14] del

20 pueblo, los hombres del campo, vestidos de limpio y despaciosos, se quedan mirándolo:

—Tien' asero...

Tiene acero[15]. Acero y plata de luna, al mismo tiempo.

_____

[10] oranges   [11] figs   [12] affectionate
[13] **igual...** the same as   [14] narrow or short streets
[15] steel

Idilio de abril

25 **L**os niños han ido con Platero al arroyo[16] de
los chopos[17], y ahora lo traen trotando, entre
juegos sin razón y risas desproporcionadas,
todo cargado de[18] flores amarillas. Allá abajo
les ha llovido —aquella nube fugaz que veló
30 el prado verde con sus **hilos** de oro y plata, en
los que tembló, como en una lira[19] de llanto[20],
el **arco iris**—. Y sobre la empapada[21] lana del
asnucho, las campanillas[22] mojadas gotean
todavía.

¡Idilio fresco, alegre, sentimental! ¡Hasta el
35 **rebuzno** de Platero se hace tierno bajo la
dulce **carga** llovida! De cuando en cuando,
vuelve la cabeza y arranca las flores a que
su bocota **alcanza.** Las campanillas, níveas[23]
y gualdas, le cuelgan[24], un momento, entre el
40 blanco babear[25] verdoso[26] y luego se le van a la
barrigota[27] cinchada. ¡Quién, como tú, Platero,
pudiera comer flores..., y que no le hicieran
daño[28]!

¡Tarde equívoca de abril!... Los ojos brillantes y
45 vivos de Platero copian toda la hora de sol
y lluvia, en cuyo ocaso[29], sobre el campo de San
Juan, se ve llover, deshilachada[30], otra nube rosa.

---

[16] stream, brook	[17] black poplars	
[18] **cargado...** loaded with	[19] lyre, a kind of harp	[20] crying, weeping
[21] soaked, drenched	[22] bellflowers	[23] snowy white
[24] hang	[25] drool, slobber	[26] greenish
[27] big belly	[28] harm	[29] sunset
[30] unraveled		

PALABRAS CLAVE

el hilo *thread*   **la carga** *load*
el arco iris *rainbow*   **alcanzar** *to reach*
el rebuzno *braying*

Repetition is a literary technique in which words and phrases are repeated for emphasis or unity. Find and circle the example of repetition in this chapter. Why do you think Juan Ramón Jiménez repeats this word? Write your answer below.

_____

_____

_____

_____

_____

A pensar...

1. How do you know that the summer is a hot one? **(Evaluate)**

_____

_____

_____

_____

2. Why does Platero bray and romp happily? **(Cause and Effect)**

_____

_____

_____

_____

Paseo

Por los hondos[31] caminos del estío[32], colgados
50 de[33] tiernas madreselvas[34], ¡cuán dulcemente
vamos! Yo leo, o canto, o digo versos al **cielo.**
Platero **mordisquea** la hierba escasa[35] de los
vallados[36] en sombra, la flor empolvada[37] de las
malvas[38], las vinagreras[39] amarillas. Está parado
55 más tiempo que andando. Yo lo dejo...

El cielo azul, azul, azul, asaeteado de mis
ojos[40] en **arrobamiento,** se levanta, sobre los
almendros[41] cargados, a sus últimas glorias.
Todo el campo, silencioso y ardiente[42], brilla[43].
60 En el río, una velita[44] blanca se eterniza, sin
viento. Hacia los montes la compacta
humareda[45] de un incendio hincha[46] sus
redondas[47] nubes negras.

---

[31] low, deep   [32] poetic word for summer
[33] **colados...** hanging from
[34] honeysuckle   [35] **hierba...** scarce grass   [36] walls, fences
[37] covered with dust   [38] mallow   [39] sorrel
[40] **asaeteado...** contemplated (fig.)   [41] almond trees
[42] glowing; blazing   [43] shines, sparkles
[44] small sail on a boat   [45] dense smoke
[46] swells, inflates   [47] round

PALABRAS CLAVE
el cielo _sky_
mordisquear _to nibble at, to take bites of_
el arrobamiento _rapture, enchantment_

Pero nuestro caminar es bien corto. Es como
65 un día suave e indefenso[48], en medio de la
vida múltiple. ¡Ni la apoteosis[49] del cielo, ni
el ultramar[50] a que va el río, ni siquiera[51] la
tragedia de las llamas[52]!

Cuando, entre un **olor** a naranjas, se oye el
70 hierro[53] alegre y fresco de la noria[54], Platero
rebuzna y **retoza** alegremente. ¡Qué sencillo
placer diario! Ya en la alberca[55], yo lleno mi
vaso y bebo aquella nieve líquida. Platero
sume[56] en el agua umbría[57] su boca,
75 y bebotea[58], aquí y allá, en lo más limpio,
avaramente[59]...

---

[48] defenseless	[49] glorification	[50] overseas
[51] **ni...** not even	[52] flames	[53] iron
[54] water wheel	[55] reservoir	[56] submerges
[57] shady	[58] drinks	[59] greedily

APUNTES

CHALLENGE Why do you
think that *Platero y yo* is called
a prose poem? Underline words
and phrases in the selection
that support your answer.
(Make Judgments)

PALABRAS CLAVE
el olor *smell*   **retozar** *to romp, to frolic*

Vocabulario de la lectura

Palabras clave

alcanzar   *to reachf*

el arco iris   *rainbow*

el arrobamiento   *rapture, enchantment*

blando(a)   *soft*

la carga   *load*

el cielo   *sky*

el hilo   *thread*

el hocico   *muzzle, snout*

mordisquear   *to nibble, to take bites of*

el olor   *smell*

el rebuzno   *braying*

retozar   *to romp, to frolic*

suave   *soft, smooth; delicate*

suelto(a)   *loose, untied*

tierno(a)   *tender, loving*

A. Escribe la **Palabra clave** que mejor complete cada oración.

1. Dejo a Platero _____ y se va al prado.

2. Platero acaricia las flores con su _____.

3. Hay un _____ después de la lluvia.

4. Platero lleva una _____ de flores.

5. Hay un _____ de naranjas en el aire.

B. Contesta cada pregunta escribiendo una de las **Palabras clave** en el espacio en blanco.

1. ¿Qué palabra tiene las cinco vocales? _____

2. ¿Qué palabra significa lo opuesto de cruel? _____

3. ¿Qué tiene nubes? _____

4. ¿Qué palabra significa jugar? _____

5. ¿Qué se puede oír? _____

¿Comprendiste?

1. ¿Cómo es Platero?

_____

_____

2. ¿Qué tiempo hace en «Idilio de abril»?

_____

3. ¿Qué hace el narrador mientras camina en «Paseo»?

_____

Conexión personal

Have you ever had a special pet? If so, describe it. If not, describe your ideal pet. What kind of animal is it? What does it look like? What does it like to do? Write your description in the notebook at the right.

Mi mascota

Para leer   *El delantal blanco*

Reading Strategy

MAKE INFERENCES ABOUT LITERATURE An inference is a logical conclusion based on evidence. It is often called "reading between the lines." Readers make inferences based on information given in the text and their own experience. You can make inferences about character, plot, setting, theme, and other aspects of a story. Practice making inferences as you read *El delantal blanco* to discover the meanings beyond the characters' spoken words. In the chart below, record lines of dialog that seem especially meaningful. Then explain what you think these remarks show.

Clave del diálogo	Inferencia
¿Y qué querías? Viniste a trabajar, no a veranear.	La Señora no respeta a La Empleada.

What You Need to Know

This reading is two excerpts from the one-act play *El delantal blanco* by Chilean playwright Sergio Vodanovic (1926–2001). The play is part of a three-part work, *Viña: tres comedias en traje de baño* (1964). It is a commentary on the artificiality of social distinctions. The play is about a society woman and her employee, who is wearing a white uniform. The bored employer suggests that they swap clothes. She wants to see how the world will look in a white apron. The employer's game will have unexpected consequences for both women.

Sobre el autor

Sergio Vodanovic (1926–2001) fue un dramaturgo chileno de descendencia croata. También fue abogado, periodista y escritor de guiones de teleseries chilenas. Además de *El delantal blanco*, escribió obras como *El senador no es honorable* (1952), *Deja que los perros ladren* (1959) y *Los fugitivos* (1965). Abordó temas psicológicos y sociales, con un enfoque especial sobre la clase media: la justicia social, el conflicto entre generaciones y las represiones sufridas por el individuo a manos de la sociedad. Vodanovic adoptó un estilo satírico, con elementos de farsa.

READING TIP The words shown in italics and parentheses are the stage directions. They are the playwright's instructions for the director, the actors, and the stage crew. They describe the props, scenery, and costumes used during a performance and tell how the characters look, move, speak, and feel.

APUNTES

El delantal blanco

Personajes
La Señora
La Empleada

La playa.

Al fondo, una carpa[1].

Frente a ella, sentadas a su sombra, **La Señora** *y* **La Empleada**.

5   **La Señora** *está en traje de baño y, sobre él, usa un blusón[2] de toalla blanca que le cubre hasta las caderas[3]. Su tez[4] está tostada por un largo veraneo[5].* **La Empleada** *viste su uniforme blanco.* **La Señora** *es una mujer de treinta años, pelo claro, rostro atrayente[6]*
10   *aunque algo duro.* **La Empleada** *tiene veinte años, tez blanca, pelo negro, rostro plácido y agradable.*

---

[1] tent   [2] smock   [3] hips   [4] complexion   [5] summer holidays
[6] attractive

READING TIP Remember the beach vocabulary that you previously learned: **playa, traje de baño, toalla, orilla, mar, arena, sol, quemar, bronceador, ola.**

APUNTES

_____

_____

_____

_____

_____

_____

CHALLENGE Why are the summer holidays coming to an end in March? **(Evaluate)**

_____

_____

_____

APUNTES

_____

_____

_____

_____

_____

_____

_____

_____

_____

La Señora. *(Gritando hacia su pequeño hijo, a quien no ve y que se supone está a la orilla del mar, justamente al borde del* **escenario.***)* ¡Alvarito!
15 ¡Alvarito! ¡No le tire[7] arena a la niñita! ¡Métase[8] al agua! Está rica… ¡Alvarito, no! ¡No le deshaga el castillo a la niñita! Juegue con ella… Sí, mi hijito… juegue…

La Empleada. Es tan peleador[9]…

20 **La Señora.** Salió al padre[10]… Es inútil corregirlo[11]. Tiene una personalidad dominante que le viene de su padre, de su abuelo, de su abuela… ¡sobre todo de su abuela!

La Empleada. ¿Vendrá el caballero[12] mañana?

25 **La Señora.** *(Se encoge de hombros[13] con* **desgano.***)* ¡No sé! Ya estamos en marzo, todas mis amigas han regresado y Álvaro me tiene todavía aburriéndome en la playa. Él dice que quiere que el niño aproveche[14] las
30 vacaciones, pero para mí que es él quien está aprovechando. *(Se saca el blusón y se tiende a tomar sol.)* ¡Sol! ¡Sol! Tres meses tomando sol. Estoy intoxicada de sol. *(Mirando inspectivamente a* **La Empleada.***)* ¿Qué haces
35 tú para no quemarte?

La Empleada. He salido tan poco de la casa…

---

[7] throw   [8] Get in   [9] quarrelsome
[10] **Salió...** He inherited his father's personality
[11] to correct or punish him
[12] the man of the house: here, the husband of **La Señora**
[13] **Se...** She shrugs her shoulders   [14] take advantage of

PALABRAS CLAVE
el escenario *stage*   el desgano *indifference*

La Señora. ¿Y qué querías? Viniste a trabajar, no a veranear. Estás recibiendo sueldo, ¿no?

La Empleada. Sí, señora. Yo sólo contestaba su
40 pregunta…

(**La Señora** *permanece tendida*[15] *recibiendo el sol.*
La Empleada *saca de una bolsa de género*[16] *una
revista de historietas fotografiadas y principia*[17] *a
leer.*)

La Señora. ¿Qué haces?

45 **La Empleada.** Leo esta revista.

La Señora. ¿La compraste tú?

La Empleada. Sí, señora.

La Señora. No se te paga tan mal, entonces, si
puedes comprarte tus revistas, ¿eh?

50 (**La Empleada** *no contesta y vuelve a mirar la revista.*)

La Señora. ¡Claro! Tú leyendo y que Alvarito
reviente[18], que se ahogue[19]…

La Empleada. Pero si está jugando con la niñita…

La Señora. Si te traje a la playa es para que
55 **vigilaras** a Alvarito y no para que te pusieras
a leer.

---

[15] **permanece…** remains lying down   [16] fabric
[17] begins   [18] dies   [19] drowns

PALABRAS CLAVE
    vigilar *to watch over, to supervise*

READER'S SUCCESS STRATEGY Use a chart like the one below to note details about each character as you read. Include physical appearance, attitudes, and behavior.

La Señora	La Empleada
tiene treinta años	tiene veinte años

APUNTES

A pensar...

What is **La Señora**'s attitude
toward **La Empleada**? (Infer)

_____

_____

_____

_____

_____

_____

CHALLENGE Why do you
think **La Señora** takes the
car to go two blocks? (**Draw
Conclusions**)

_____

_____

_____

_____

_____

_____

APUNTES

_____

_____

_____

_____

_____

_____

_____

_____

(**La Empleada** *deja la revista y se incorpora*[20] *para ir
donde está Alvarito.*)

La Señora. ¡No! Lo puedes vigilar desde aquí.
60 Quédate a mi lado, pero observa al niño.
¿Sabes? Me gusta venir contigo a la playa.

La Empleada. ¿Por qué?

La Señora. Bueno… no sé… Será por lo mismo
que me gusta venir en el auto, aunque la casa
65 esté a dos cuadras. Me gusta que vean el auto.
Todos los días, hay alguien que se para al lado
de él y lo mira y comenta. No cualquiera[21]
tiene un auto como el de nosotros… Claro,
tú no te das cuenta de la diferencia. Estás
70 demasiado acostumbrada a lo bueno…
Dime… ¿Cómo es tu casa?

La Empleada. Yo no tengo casa.

La Señora. No habrás nacido empleada,
supongo. Tienes que haberte criado[22] en
75 alguna parte, debes haber tenido padres…
¿Eres del campo?

La Empleada. Sí.

La Señora. Y tuviste ganas de conocer la ciudad,
¿ah?

80 **La Empleada.** No. Me gustaba allá.

---

[20] sits up   [21] **No...** Not just anybody
[22] grown up

La Señora. ¿Por qué te viniste, entonces?

La Empleada. Tenía que trabajar.

La Señora. No me vengas con ese cuento.
Conozco la vida de los inquilinos[23] en el
85 campo. Lo pasan bien. Les regalan una cuadra[24]
para que cultiven. Tienen alimentos gratis[25]
y hasta les sobra[26] para vender. Algunos
tienen hasta sus vaquitas… ¿Tus padres tenían
vacas?

90 **La Empleada.** Sí, señora. Una.

La Señora. ¿Ves? ¿Qué más quieren? ¡Alvarito!
¡No se meta tan allá, que puede venir una ola!
¿Qué edad tienes?

La Empleada. ¿Yo?

95 **La Señora.** A ti te estoy hablando. No estoy loca
para hablar sola.

La Empleada. Ando en los veintiuno[27]…

La Señora. ¡Veintiuno! A los veintiuno yo me
casé. ¿No has pensado en casarte?

100 (**La Empleada** *baja la vista y no contesta.*)

---

[23] Chilean word for tenant farmers   [24] piece of land   [25] free
[26] is left over   [27] **Ando...** I'm around 21 years old

CHALLENGE Do you think
that **La Señora**'s description
of the lives of tenant farmers
is accurate? Why or why not?
(**Draw Conclusions**)

APUNTES

CHALLENGE Do you think that **La Empleada** is happy working for **La Señora**? Explain your answer. **(Infer)**

_____

_____

_____

_____

_____

APUNTES

_____

_____

_____

_____

_____

_____

_____

_____

_____

CHALLENGE Read the boxed text. What does **La Señora** think about money? Do you agree with her? Write your answer on the lines below. **(Analyze)**

_____

_____

_____

_____

_____

_____

_____

_____

La Señora. ¡Las cosas que se me ocurre preguntar! ¿Para qué querrías casarte? En la casa tienes de todo: comida, una buena pieza[28], **delantales** limpios… Y si te casaras… ¿Qué es

105 lo que tendrías? Te llenarías de chiquillos[29], no más.

La Empleada. _(Como para sí[30].)_ Me gustaría casarme.

La Señora. ¡Tonterías[31]! Cosas que se te ocurren

110 por leer historias de amor en las revistas baratas… Acuérdate de esto: los príncipes azules[32] ya no existen. No es el color lo que importa, sino el bolsillo[33]. Cuando mis padres no me aceptaban un pololo[34] porque

115 no tenía plata[35], yo me indignaba, pero llegó Álvaro con sus industrias y sus fundos[36] y no quedaron contentos hasta que lo casaron conmigo. A mí no me gustaba porque era gordo y tenía la costumbre de sorberse los

120 mocos[37], pero después en el matrimonio, uno se acostumbra a todo. Y llega a la conclusión que todo da lo mismo[38], salvo[39] la plata. Sin la plata no somos nada. Yo tengo plata, tú no tienes. Ésa es toda la diferencia entre nosotras. ¿No te parece?

125 **La Empleada.** Sí, pero…

---

[28] room   [29] children   [30] **Como…** As if to herself
[31] Nonsense!   [32] **príncipes…** perfect men of romantic stories
[33] purse, money   [34] Chilean word for _boyfriend_   [35] money
[36] rural properties   [37] **soberse…** to sniffle or snuffle
[38] **da…** is all the same, has the same importance
[39] except (for)

PALABRAS CLAVE
el delantal _apron_

La Señora. ¡Ah! Lo crees, ¿eh? Pero es mentira. Hay algo que es más importante que la plata: la clase. Eso no se compra. Se tiene o no se tiene. Álvaro no tiene clase. Yo sí la tengo. Y
130 podría vivir en una pocilga[40] y todos se darían cuenta de que soy alguien. No una cualquiera. Alguien. Te das cuenta, ¿verdad?

La Empleada. Sí, señora.

(···)

La Señora. Mira. Se me ha ocurrido algo.
135 Préstame tu delantal.

La Empleada. ¿Cómo?

La Señora. Préstame tu delantal.

La Empleada. Pero… ¿Para qué?

La Señora. Quiero ver cómo se ve el mundo,
140 qué apariencia tiene la playa cuando se la ve encerrada[41] en un delantal de empleada.

La Empleada. ¿Ahora?

La Señora. Sí, ahora.

La Empleada. Pero es que… No tengo un vestido
145 debajo.

---

[40] pigsty, pigpen   [41] confined

MÁRCALO ANÁLISIS

Hyperbole is a figure of speech in which exaggeration is used for emphasis or effect, as in *This book weighs a ton*. Find and underline an example of hyperbole on this page.

A pensar…

1. Why do you think the playwright doesn't give the two women names? **(Make Judgments)**

2. Why do you think **La Señora** uses the **usted** forms of verbs with her son but the **tú** forms with **La Empleada**? Why does **La Empleada** use **usted** forms with **La Señora**? **(Infer)**

APUNTES

A pensar...

What is your opinion of the two women so far? (**Make Judgments**)

_____

_____

_____

_____

_____

APUNTES

_____

_____

_____

_____

_____

_____

_____

_____

_____

_____

La Señora. *(Tirándole el blusón.)* Toma… Ponte esto.

La Empleada. Voy a quedar en calzones[42]…

La Señora. Es lo suficientemente largo como
150 para cubrirte. Y en todo caso vas a mostrar menos que lo que mostrabas con los trajes de baño que arrendabas[43] en Cartagena. *(Se levanta y obliga a levantarse a **La Empleada**.)* Ya. Métete en la carpa y cámbiate. (Prácticamente
155 *obliga a **La Empleada** a entrar a la carpa y luego lanza al interior de ella el blusón de toalla. Se dirige al primer plano[44] y le habla a su hijo.)*

La Señora. Alvarito, métase un poco al agua. Mójese las patitas siquiera… No sea tan de
160 rulo[45]… ¡Eso es! ¿Ves que es rica el agüita? *(Se vuelve hacia la carpa y habla hacia dentro de ella.)* ¿Estás lista? *(Entra a la carpa.)*

*Después de un instante, sale **La Empleada** vestida con el blusón de toalla. Se ha prendido[46] el pelo
165 hacia atrás y su aspecto ya difiere algo de la tímida muchacha que conocemos. Con dedicadeza se tiende de bruces[47] sobre la arena. Sale **La Señora** abotonándose aún su delantal blanco. Se va a sentar delante de **La Empleada**, pero vuelve un poco
170 más atrás.*

---

[42] underwear   [43] you rented   [44] foreground   [45] like unirrigated land
[46] pinned   [47] face-down

La Señora. No. Adelante no. Una empleada en la playa se sienta siempre un poco más atrás que su patrona. (*Se sienta sobre sus pantorrillas*[48] *y mira, divertida, en todas direcciones.*)

175 **La Empleada** *cambia de postura con* **displicencia.** **La Señora** *toma la revista de* **La Empleada** *y principia a leerla. Al principio, hay una sonrisa irónica en sus labios*[49] *que desaparece luego al interesarse por la lectura. Al leer mueve los labios.* **La Empleada,** 180 *con naturalidad, toma de la bolsa de playa de* **La Señora** *un frasco*[50] *de aceite bronceador y principia a extenderlo con lentitud por sus piernas.* **La Señora** *la ve. Intenta una reacción* **reprobatoria,** *pero queda desconcertada.*

185 **La Señora.** ¿Qué haces?

La Empleada *no contesta.* **La Señora** *opta por seguir la lectura, vigilando de vez en vez con la vista lo que hace* **La Empleada.** *Ésta ahora se ha sentado y se mira detenidamente*[51] *las uñas*[52].

190 **La Señora.** ¿Por qué te miras las uñas?

La Empleada. Tengo que arreglármelas.

La Señora. Nunca te había visto antes mirarte las uñas.

La Empleada. No se me había ocurrido.

---

[48] calves   [49] lips   [50] small bottle   [51] thoroughly, closely
[52] fingernails

PALABRAS CLAVE
   la displicencia   *apathy, lack of interest*
   reprobatorio(a)   *condemning, disapproving*

⫿⫿⫿ MÁRCALO ⟩ ANÁLISIS
Irony is the contrast between what is expected and what actually exists or happens. In this play, the irony is in the role reversal between employer and employee in which **La Empleada** says and does things that **La Señora** would normally say and do and vice versa. For example, **La Señora** takes **La Empleada**'s magazine and starts to read it with interest after ridiculing it before they swapped clothes. Find and underline examples of irony in the dialog of this section of the play.

CHALLENGE What else changes besides their appearance when the two characters swap clothes? **(Evaluate)**

_____
_____
_____
_____
_____

APUNTES

_____
_____
_____
_____
_____
_____

195 **La Señora.** Este delantal acalora[53].

La Empleada. Son los mejores y los más durables.

La Señora. Lo sé. Yo los compré.

La Empleada. Le queda bien.

La Señora. *(Divertida.)* Y tú no te ves nada de
200 mal con esa tenida[54]. *(Se ríe.)* Cualquiera se
equivocaría. Más de un jovencito te podría
hacer la corte[55]… ¡Sería como para contarlo!

La Empleada. Alvarito se está metiendo muy
adentro. Vaya a vigilarlo.

205 **La Señora.** *(Se levanta inmediatamente y se
adelanta.)* ¡Alvarito! ¡Alvarito! No se vaya tan
adentro… Puede venir una ola. (***Recapacita**
de pronto y se vuelve desconcertada hacia **La Empleada.**)

La Señora. ¿Por qué no fuiste tú?

210 **La Empleada.** ¿Adónde?

La Señora. ¿Por qué me dijiste que yo fuera a
vigilar a Alvarito?

La Empleada. *(Con naturalidad.)* Usted lleva el
delantal blanco.

215 **La Señora.** Te gusta el juego, ¿ah?

CHALLENGE Read the boxed
text. Why do you think **La
Señora** is disconcerted? **(Draw
Conclusions)**

---

[53] makes one hot   [54] Chilean word for *uniform* or *suit*
[55] **hacer…** to court

PALABRAS CLAVE
   recapacitar   *to reconsider, to mull over*

Una pelota de goma[56], impulsada por un niño que juega cerca, ha caído a los pies de **La Empleada**. *Ella la mira y no hace ningún movimiento. Luego mira a* **La Señora.** *Ésta, instintivamente, se dirige a*
220 *la pelota y la tira en la dirección en que vino.*
La Empleada *busca en la bolsa de playa de* **La Señora** *y se pone sus anteojos para el sol.*

La Señora. (*Molesta.*) ¿Quién te ha autorizado para que uses mis anteojos?

225 **La Empleada.** ¿Cómo se ve la playa vestida con un delantal blanco?

La Señora. Es **gracioso.** ¿Y tú? ¿Cómo ves la playa ahora?

La Empleada. Es gracioso.

230 **La Señora.** (*Molesta.*) ¿Dónde está la gracia?

La Empleada. En que no hay diferencia.

La Señora. ¿Cómo?

La Empleada. Usted con el delantal blanco es la empleada; yo con este blusón y los anteojos
235 oscuros soy la señora.

La Señora. ¿Cómo?... ¿Cómo **te atreves** a decir eso?

---
[56] rubber

PALABRAS CLAVE
molesto(a) *bothered, annoyed*   **atreverse** *to dare*
gracioso(a) *amusing, funny*

READING TIP A compound word is the combination of two different words to make a new one. You can figure out the meaning of a compound word by knowing the meaning of the words that form it. On this page, the word **anteojos** is a combination of the words **ante** (before) and **ojos** (eyes). What do you think it means? What other word do you know that means the same thing?

APUNTES

A pensar...

What role do you think clothes play in determining how people act? **(Make Judgments)**

_____

_____

_____

_____

_____

_____

_____

APUNTES

_____

_____

_____

_____

_____

_____

_____

CHALLENGE How and why does the way the characters speak to each other change? Highlight the lines where this happens. **(Analyze)**

_____

_____

_____

_____

_____

_____

_____

_____

_____

La Empleada. ¿Se habría molestado en **recoger** la pelota si no estuviese[57] vestida de empleada?

240 **La Señora.** Estamos jugando.

La Empleada. ¿Cuándo?

La Señora. Ahora.

La Empleada. ¿Y antes?

La Señora. ¿Antes?

245 **La Empleada.** Sí. Cuando yo estaba vestida de empleada.

La Señora. Eso no es juego. Es la realidad.

La Empleada. ¿Por qué?

La Señora. Porque sí.

250 **La Empleada.** Un juego… un juego más largo… como el «pacoladrón[58]». A unos les corresponde ser «pacos», a otros «ladrones».

La Señora. _(Indignada.)_ ¡Usted se está insolentando!

La Empleada. ¡No me grites! ¡La insolente eres tú!

_____

[57] weren't   [58] cops and robbers

PALABRAS CLAVE
  recoger   _to pick up, to retrieve_

255 **La Señora.** ¿Qué significa eso? ¿Usted me está **tuteando**?

La Empleada. ¿Y acaso tú no me tratas de tú?

La Señora. ¿Yo?

La Empleada. Sí.

260 **La Señora.** ¡**Basta** ya! ¡Se acabó este juego!

La Empleada. ¡A mí me gusta!

La Señora. ¡Se acabó! *(Se acerca violentamente a* **La Empleada.***)*

La Empleada. *(Firme.)* ¡Retírese[59]!

265 *(***La Señora** *se detiene sorprendida.)*

La Señora. ¿Te has vuelto loca?

La Empleada. Me he vuelto señora.

La Señora. Te puedo **despedir** en cualquier momento.

270 **La Empleada.** *(Explota en grandes **carcajadas**, como si lo que hubiera[60] oído fuera el chiste más gracioso que jamás ha escuchado.)*

---

[59] Move back   [60] had

PALABRAS CLAVE

tutear *to address as **tú***	**despedir** *to dismiss, to fire*
bastar *to be enough*	**la carcajada** *guffaw, loud laughter*

A pensar...

Why do you think the play is called *El delantal blanco*? What is the apron a symbol of? **(Infer)**

_____

_____

_____

_____

_____

_____

CHALLENGE How do you think the play will end? Write your prediction on the lines below. **(Predict)**

_____

_____

_____

_____

_____

_____

_____

_____

Vocabulario de la lectura

Palabras clave

atreverse *to dare*

bastar *to be enough*

la carcajada *guffaw, loud laughter*

el delantal *apron*

el desgano *indifference*

despedir *to dismiss, to fire*

la displicencia *apathy, lack of interest*

el escenario *stage*

gracioso(a) *amusing, funny*

molesto(a) *bothered, annoyed*

recapacitar *to reconsider, to mull over*

recoger *to pick up, to retrieve*

reprobatorio(a) *condemning, disapproving*

tutear *to address as **tú***

vigilar *to watch over, to supervise*

A. Para cada palabra de la primera columna, busca la definición en la segunda columna. Escribe la letra de la definición correcta en el espacio en blanco.

_____ 1. bastar

_____ 2. vigilar

_____ 3. carcajada

_____ 4. escenario

_____ 5. despedir

A. risa incontenible

B. ser suficiente

C. echar a alguien de un trabajo

D. observar atentamente a alguien

E. lugar del teatro en que se actúa

B. Escribe la **Palabra clave** que complete cada frase.

1. el _____ blanco

2. al borde del _____

3. una reacción _____

4. un chiste _____

5. _____ la pelota

¿Comprendiste?

1. ¿De dónde es **La Empleada**? ¿Por qué salió de allí?

_____

_____

2. ¿Por qué a **La Señora** no le gustaba su esposo? ¿Por qué se casó con él?

_____

_____

3. ¿Por qué quiere **La Señora** que **La Empleada** le preste el delantal?

_____

_____

4. ¿Dónde se sienta **La Señora** después de ponerse el delantal? ¿Por qué?

_____

_____

5. ¿Por qué le dice **La Empleada** a **La Señora** que vigile a Alvarito?

_____

_____

Conexión personal

Do you have any clothes that make you feel different when you wear them? What are they? Describe them. How do they make you feel when you are wearing them? Write your answer in the notebook at the right.

La ropa especial

_____

_____

_____

_____

_____

_____

Para leer *La casa de los espíritus*

Reading Strategy

UNDERSTAND CHARACTERS' MOTIVES Motives are the emotions, wants, or needs that cause a character to act or react in a certain way. As you read this excerpt from *La casa de los espíritus*, use the chart below to understand the actions of the main characters. Next to each action, describe the reason, or motivation, the character had for taking it.

Acción	Razón
1. Esteban Trueba pide ser recibido en la casa de la familia del Valle.	
2. Esteban pide autorización para visitar a Clara del Valle de nuevo.	
3. Clara le pregunta a Esteban si él quiere casarse con ella.	
4. Clara está dispuesta a casarse con Esteban.	

What You Need to Know

This reading in an excerpt from the novel *La casa de los espíritus (The House of the Spirits)* by Chilean writer Isabel Allende. It was originally published in Spain in 1982. The novel narrates the history of several generations of the Trueba family in Chile. Esteban Trueba had been in love with and engaged to marry Rosa, the oldest daughter of the del Valle family. The youngest daughter, Clara, is clairvoyant and announced that there would be a death in the house. Rosa died shortly afterward, and Clara didn't speak again for nine years. Her silence was broken on her nineteenth birthday with the announcement that she was going to marry Rosa's fiancé. Two months later, Esteban Trueba appears.

Sobre la autora

Hija de padre chileno diplomático, Isabel Allende (1942–) nació en Lima, Perú, y se crió en Santiago de Chile. Participó en la oposición al régimen militar establecido en Chile después de la muerte de Salvador Allende, presidente del país y primo del padre de la autora. Como resultado, ella tuvo que salir al exilio. Vive actualmente en California. Es periodista, novelista y cuentista. Entre sus obras más conocidas están *La casa de los espíritus* (1982), *Cuentos de Eva Luna* (1989) y *Paula* (1994).

~~~~~~~~~~

La casa de los espíritus

El día que Esteban Trueba pidió ser recibido, Severo y Nívea del Valle recordaron las palabras con que Clara había roto su larga **mudez,** de modo que[1] no manifestaron
5 ninguna **extrañeza** cuando el visitante les preguntó si tenían alguna hija en edad y condición de casarse. Sacaron sus cuentas y le informaron que Ana se había metido a monja[2], Teresa estaba muy enferma y todas
10 las demás estaban casadas, menos Clara, la menor, que aún estaba **disponible,** pero era una criatura algo **estrafalaria,** poco apta[3] para las responsabilidades matrimoniales y

---

[1] **de...** so that
[2] **se...** had become a nun   [3] fit

PALABRAS CLAVE
la mudez   *silence; muteness*
la extrañeza   *surprise, astonishment*
disponible   *available*
estrafalario(a)   *eccentric*

READING TIP Isabel Allende writes very long sentences and paragraphs. Try breaking long sentences into smaller sections as you read. Often, a comma will set off a section of a sentence.
APUNTES

LITERATURA ADICIONAL

READER'S SUCCESS STRATEGY *La casa de los espíritus* is an example of magic realism, in which the real and the fantastic are mixed together. The setting or characters might have magical or extraordinary qualities. As you read, find and highlight words and phrases that indicate the fantastic in the novel.

A pensar...

1. Why didn't Clara speak for so long? Circle the correct answer. **(Clarify)**

She couldn't.

She didn't want to.

She had nothing to say.

2. Why do you think Clara's parents tell Esteban all of her idiosyncrasies? **(Draw Conclusions)**

_____

_____

_____

_____

_____

APUNTES

_____

_____

_____

_____

_____

_____

_____

_____

la vida doméstica. Con toda honestidad, le
15 contaron las **rarezas** de su hija menor, sin
omitir el hecho de que había permanecido
sin hablar durante la mitad de su existencia,
porque no le daba la gana hacerlo y no porque
no pudiera, como había aclarado muy bien
20 el rumano Rostipov y confirmado el doctor
Cuevas con innumerables exámenes. Pero
Esteban Trueba no era hombre de dejarse
amedrentar[4] por historias de fantasmas[5] que
deambulan[6] por los corredores, por objetos
25 que se mueven a la distancia con el poder
de la mente o por **presagios** de mala suerte,
y mucho menos por el prolongado silencio,
que consideraba una virtud. Concluyó que
ninguna de esas cosas eran inconvenientes
30 para echar hijos sanos y legítimos al mundo
y pidió conocer a Clara. Nívea salió a buscar
a su hija y los dos hombres quedaron solos
en el salón, ocasión que Trueba, con su
franqueza habitual, aprovechó para plantear
35 sin preámbulos[7] su solvencia económica.

—¡Por favor, no se adelante[8], Esteban!
—le interrumpió Severo—. Primero tiene
que ver a la niña, conocerla mejor, y también
tenemos que considerar los deseos de Clara.
40 ¿No le parece?

_____

[4] become frightened or scared [5] ghosts [6] wander, roam
[7] **sin...** without further ado [8] get ahead of yourself

PALABRAS CLAVE
la rareza *idiosyncrasy, peculiarity* **el presagio** *omen; premonition*

Nívea regresó con Clara. La joven entró al salón con las mejillas arreboladas[9] y las uñas negras, porque había estado ayudando al jardinero a plantar papas de dalias y en esa
45 ocasión le falló la **clarividencia** para esperar al futuro novio con un arreglo más **esmerado.** Al verla, Esteban se puso de pie **asombrado.** La recordaba como una criatura flaca[10] y asmática, sin la menor gracia, pero la joven
50 que tenía al frente era un delicado medallón de marfil[11], con un rostro dulce y una mata de cabello[12] castaño, crespo[13] y desordenado escapándose en rizos del peinado, ojos melancólicos, que se transformaban en una
55 expresión burlona[14] y chispeante[15] cuando se reía, con una risa franca y abierta, la cabeza ligeramente inclinada hacia atrás. Ella lo saludó con un apretón de manos[16], sin dar muestras de timidez.

60 —Lo estaba esperando —dijo sencillamente.

Transcurrieron un par de horas en visita de cortesía, hablando de la temporada lírica, los viajes a Europa, la situación política y los resfríos de invierno, bebiendo mistela
65 y comiendo pasteles de hojaldre[17]. Esteban observaba a Clara con toda la discreción de

---

[9] reddened cheeks [10] skinny [11] ivory
[12] **mata...** head of hair [13] frizzy [14] joking, mocking
[15] sparkling [16] **apretón...** handshake
[17] **pasteles...** puff pastry

PALABRAS CLAVE

la clarividencia *clairvoyance*   asombrado(a) *amazed, astonished*
esmerado(a) *polished*

MÁRCALO > ANÁLISIS
Remember that a metaphor is the direct comparison of one thing with another. Find and circle the metaphor on this page.

CHALLENGE Why is Esteban amazed when he sees Clara? **(Summarize)**

_____

_____

_____

_____

APUNTES

_____

_____

_____

_____

_____

_____

_____

_____

_____

_____

||| MÁRCALO > **ANÁLISIS**

Flashback is inserting an earlier event into the normal chronological order of a narrative. Isabel Allende uses flashbacks to remind readers of earlier events and characters in the novel. Find and underline the sentence with the flashback that Esteban has about Rosa.

APUNTES

_____

_____

_____

_____

_____

_____

_____

_____

_____

_____

_____

_____

CHALLENGE Why is Clara's mother horrified when Clara asks Esteban if he wants to marry her? **(Infer)**

_____

_____

_____

_____

que era capaz, sintiéndose paulatinamente[18] seducido por la muchacha. No recordaba haber estado tan interesado en alguien desde

70 el día glorioso en que vio a Rosa, la bella, comprando caramelos de anís en la confitería[19] de la Plaza de Armas. Comparó a las dos hermanas y llegó a la conclusión de que Clara aventajaba[20] en simpatía, aunque Rosa, sin

75 duda, había sido mucho más hermosa. Cayó la noche y entraron dos empleadas a correr las cortinas[21] y encender las luces, entonces Esteban se dio cuenta que su visita había durado demasiado. Sus **modales** dejaban

80 mucho que desear. Saludó rígidamente a Severo y Nívea y pidió autorización para visitar a Clara de nuevo.

—Espero no aburrirla, Clara —dijo sonrojándose[22]—. Soy un hombre **rudo,**

85 de campo, y soy por lo menos quince años mayor. No sé tratar a una joven como usted...

—¿Usted quiere casarse conmigo? —preguntó Clara y él notó un brillo[23] irónico en sus pupilas de avellana[24].

90 —¡Clara, por Dios! —exclamó su madre horrorizada—. Disculpe, Esteban, esta niña siempre ha sido muy impertinente.

---

[18] gradually, little by little   [19] candy shop   [20] was ahead
[21] **correr...** to draw the curtains   [22] blushing
[23] glitter, shine   [24] hazel(nut)

PALABRAS CLAVE
los modales _manners_   **rudo(a)** _crude, unpolished_

—Quiero saberlo, mamá, para no perder tiempo —dijo Clara.

95 —A mí también me gustan las cosas directas —sonrió feliz Esteban—. Sí, Clara, a eso he venido.

Clara lo tomó del brazo y lo acompañó hasta la salida. En la última mirada que
100 intercambiaron Esteban comprendió que lo había aceptado y lo invadió la alegría. Al tomar el coche, iba sonriendo sin poder creer en su buena suerte y sin saber por qué una joven tan **encantadora** como Clara lo
105 había aceptado sin conocerlo. No sabía que ella había visto su propio destino, por eso lo había llamado con el pensamiento y estaba dispuesta a[25] casarse sin amor.

---

[25] **estaba...** was prepared to

A pensar...

Why does Esteban want to get married? Why does Clara agree to marry Esteban? **(Summarize)**

APUNTES

PALABRAS CLAVE
encantador(a) *enchanting, charming*

Vocabulario de la lectura

Palabras clave

asombrado(a) *amazed, astonished*

la clarividencia *clairvoyance*

disponible *available*

encantador(a) *enchanting, charming*

esmerado(a) *polished*

estrafalario(a) *eccentric*

la extrañeza *surprise, astonishment*

los modales *manners*

la mudez *silence; muteness*

el presagio *omen; premonition*

la rareza *idiosyncrasy, peculiarity*

rudo(a) *crude, unpolished*

A. Completa cada espacio en blanco con un sinónimo (o palabra con un significado similar) de la lista de **Palabras clave.**

1. maneras _____

2. predicción _____

3. sorpresa _____

4. libre _____

5. silencio _____

B. Escribe un párrafo corto sobre el personaje de Clara. Usa por lo menos cuatro de las **Palabras clave** en tu descripción.

_____

_____

_____

_____

_____

_____

_____

¿Comprendiste?

1. ¿Qué les preguntó Esteban Trueba a Severo y Nívea del Valle?

_____

2. ¿Qué le informaron Severo y Nívea del Valle?

_____

_____

3. ¿Cómo recordaba Esteban a Clara?

_____

4. ¿Cómo comparó Esteban a Clara con su hermana Rosa?

_____

_____

5. ¿Por qué le preguntó Clara a Esteban si él quería casarse con ella?

_____

Conexión personal

Have you ever known someone eccentric? Describe that person. What are his or her idiosyncrasies: a unique style of dress, strange collections, odd habits? Write your description in the notebook at the right.

> Conozco a una persona estrafalaria
> que se llama...
> _____
> _____
> _____
> _____
> _____
> _____
> _____
> _____

Academic and Informational Reading

In this section you'll find strategies to help you read all kinds of informational materials. The examples here range from magazines you read for fun to textbooks to schedules. Applying these simple and effective techniques will help you be a successful reader of the many texts you encounter every day.

Reading a Magazine Article

A magazine article is designed to catch and hold your interest. Learning how to recognize the items on a magazine page will help you read even the most complicated articles. Look at the sample magazine article as you read each strategy below.

A Read the **title** and other **headings** to get an idea of what the article is about. The title often presents the article's main topic. Smaller headings may introduce subtopics related to the main topic.

B Note introductory text that is set off in some way, such as an **indented paragraph** or a passage in a **different typeface.** This text often summarizes the article.

C Pay attention to terms in **quotation marks, italics,** or **boldface.** Look for definitions before or after these terms.

D Study **visuals**—photos, pictures, charts, or maps. Visuals enrich the text and help bring the topic to life.

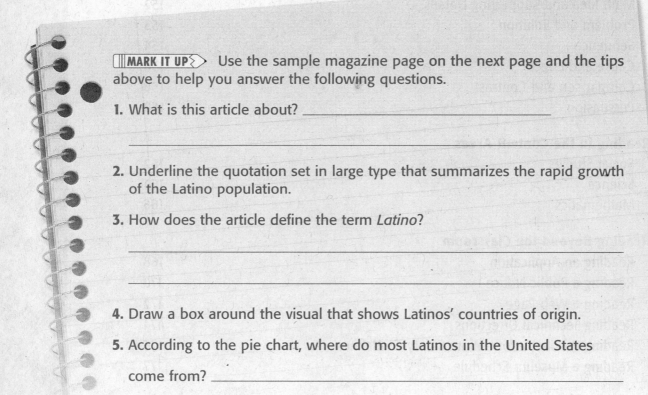

MARK IT UP Use the sample magazine page on the next page and the tips above to help you answer the following questions.

1. What is this article about? _____

_____

2. Underline the quotation set in large type that summarizes the rapid growth of the Latino population.

3. How does the article define the term *Latino*?

_____

_____

4. Draw a box around the visual that shows Latinos' countries of origin.

5. According to the pie chart, where do most Latinos in the United States

come from? _____

A Latino Population Soars

Latinos are on the move. Between 1990 and 2002, the Latino population in the United States skyrocketed—from 22.4 million to 38.5 million. That's more than the total population of Argentina or Spain! Latinos now represent over 13% of U.S. residents, and experts predict that by 2050, one-fourth of all Americans will be of Latino origin.

> **B** "By 2050, one-fourth of all Americans will be of Latino origin."

The term *Latino* refers to people **C** of Spanish-speaking origin from Latin America. Although most Latinos in the United States are from Mexico, Puerto Rico, or Cuba, approximately 17 different countries of origin are represented.

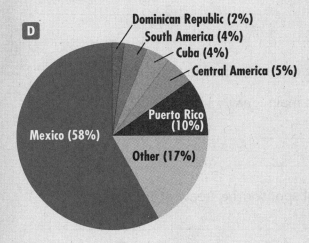

D

Dominican Republic (2%)
South America (4%)
Cuba (4%)
Central America (5%)
Puerto Rico (10%)
Mexico (58%)
Other (17%)

Where Latinos in the U.S. Come From

Not only are the numbers of Latinos in the United States increasing steadily, but they also include a greater percentage of young people than in the Anglo population. Nearly 45% of Latinos are under ten years of age, compared with only 27% of Anglos.

Although immigration played an important role in swelling the Latino population during the 1980s and 1990s, times are changing. According to a leading Spanish-language publication, almost one in four Latinos has at least one parent who was born outside the United States. For one in five Latinos, both parents were born in the United States.

Until recently, most Latinos settled in the western or southwestern states. Their numbers have been increasing all across the country, however. The numbers of Latinos in eight states—California, Texas, Arizona, Nevada, Colorado, Florida, New York, and New Jersey—is at or above the 13% national average. New Mexico tops the charts, though, with Latinos accounting for 42% of the state's citizens.

Latinos have contributed greatly to their new home. They have growing economic influence and are increasingly represented in positions of power in politics, business, and education.

Reading a Textbook

The first page of a textbook lesson introduces you to a particular topic. The page also provides important information that will guide you through the rest of the lesson. Look at the sample textbook page as you read each strategy below.

A Preview the **title** and other **headings** to find out the lesson's main topic and related subtopics.

B Read the list of **main idea, objectives,** or **focus.** These items summarize the lesson and set the purpose for your reading.

C Look for a list of terms or **vocabulary words.** These words will be identified and defined throughout the lesson.

D Find words set in special type, such as **italics** or **boldface.** Also look for material in parentheses. Boldface is often used to identify the vocabulary terms in a lesson.

E Notice text that is set off in some way on the page, such as in a tinted box. This material may be from a **primary source** or a **quotation** that gives firsthand knowledge or perspective on a topic.

F Examine **visuals,** such as photographs, illustrations, charts, maps, time lines, and their **captions.** Visuals can add information and interest to the topic.

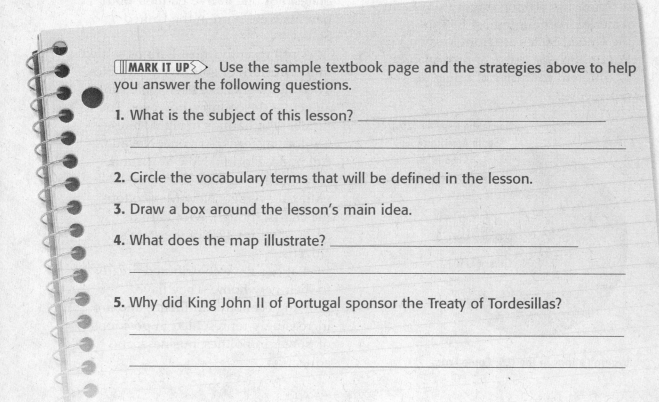

MARK IT UP Use the sample textbook page and the strategies above to help you answer the following questions.

1. What is the subject of this lesson? _____

_____

2. Circle the vocabulary terms that will be defined in the lesson.

3. Draw a box around the lesson's main idea.

4. What does the map illustrate? _____

_____

5. Why did King John II of Portugal sponsor the Treaty of Tordesillas?

_____

_____

1 Spain Claims an Empire

TERMS & NAMES
Treaty of
   Tordesillas
missionary
mercantilism
Amerigo Vespucci
conquistador
Hernando Cortés
Montezuma
Francisco Pizarro

MAIN IDEA

Spain claimed a large empire in the Americas.

WHY IT MATTERS NOW

The influence of Spanish culture remains strong in modern America.

ONE EUROPEAN'S STORY

Pope Alexander VI had an important decision to make. In 1493, the rulers of Spain and Portugal wanted him to decide who would control the lands that European sailors were exploring. Ferdinand and Isabella of Spain expected Alexander VI to give Spain the rights over many of these lands. But King John II of Portugal claimed territories, too. What would the new pope do?

In May 1493, Alexander VI issued his ruling. He drew an imaginary line around the world. It was called the Line of Demarcation. Portugal could claim all non-Christian lands to the east of the line. Spain could claim the non-Christian lands to the west. In this section, you will learn how Spain and Portugal led Europe in the race to gain colonies in the Americas.

Pope Alexander VI

Treaty of Tordesillas (1494)

Line of Demarcation (1493)

A Spain and Portugal Compete

King John II was unhappy with the pope's placement of the line. He believed that it favored Spain. So he demanded that the Spanish rulers meet with him to change the pope's decision. In June 1494, the two countries agreed to the **Treaty of Tordesillas** (TAWR•day•SEEL•yahs). This treaty moved the Line of Demarcation more than 800 miles farther west.

The change eventually allowed Portugal to claim much of eastern South America, which later became the Portuguese colony of Brazil. After making this agreement, Spain and Portugal increased their voyages of exploration in search of wealth, power, and glory.

European countries had three main goals during this age of exploration. First, they wanted to spread Christianity beyond Europe. Each expedition included **missionaries,** or people sent to convert the native peoples to Christianity. Second, they wanted to expand their empires. Third, they wanted to become rich.

By increasing their wealth, European countries could gain power and security. An economic system called **mercantilism** describes how

European Exploration of the Americas **61**

Reading a Graph

Graphs are used to present information visually. Different kinds of graphs include bar graphs, circle or pie graphs, and line graphs. A *bar graph* compares one or more characteristics of several items. The following tips can help you read a bar graph quickly and accurately. As you read each tip, look at the bar graph on this page.

A Look at the **title** to find out what the graph is about.

B Read the **labels** on the **vertical axis** (up and down) and the **horizontal axis** (side to side) to find out what kind of information is shown.

C Study the **visual pattern** created by the elements in the graph. Which is the tallest? Which is the shortest? What is the relationship between the elements?

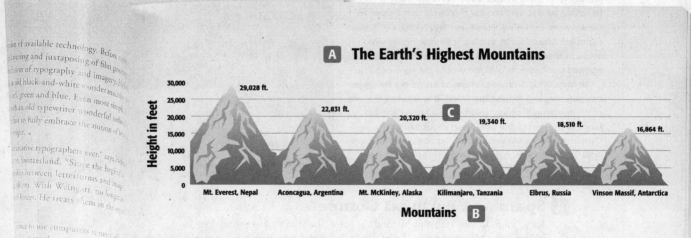

A The Earth's Highest Mountains

MARK IT UP Answer the following questions using the bar graph and the tips above.

1. What is the title of this graph?

_____

2. What information is provided on the vertical axis?

_____

3. Which mountain is located in South America?

_____

4. How much higher is Mt. Everest than the next highest mountain in the graph?

_____

Reading a Map

To read a map correctly, you have to identify and understand its elements. Look at the example below as you read each strategy in this list.

A Scan the **title** to understand the content of the map.

B Study the **legend,** or **key,** to find out what symbols and colors on the map stand for.

C Look at **geographic labels** to understand specific places on the map.

D Locate the **compass rose,** or **pointer,** to determine direction.

E Check the **scale** to understand how distance is represented on the map.

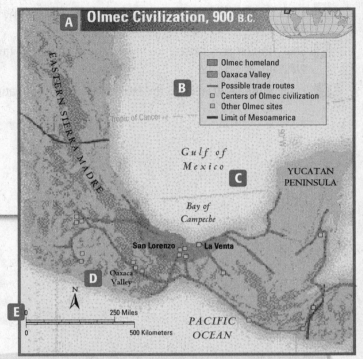

A Olmec Civilization, 900 B.C.

B
- Olmec homeland
- Oaxaca Valley
- Possible trade routes
- Centers of Olmec civilization
- Other Olmec sites
- Limit of Mesoamerica

EASTERN SIERRA MADRE

Tropic of Cancer

Gulf of Mexico

C

YUCATAN PENINSULA

Bay of Campeche

San Lorenzo   La Venta

D Oaxaca Valley

N

E 0   250 Miles
0   500 Kilometers

PACIFIC OCEAN

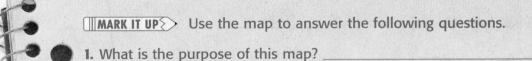

MARK IT UP Use the map to answer the following questions.

1. What is the purpose of this map? _____

_____

2. How many centers of Olmec civilization or other Olmec sites were located inside the Olmec homeland?

_____

3. What relationship does the map show between Olmec sites and trade routes?

_____

4. Draw a straight line from the northern to the southern limit of Mesoamerica. About how many kilometers long was this region?

_____

Reading a Diagram

Diagrams combine pictures with a few words to provide a lot of information. Look at the example on the opposite page as you read each of the following strategies.

A Look at the **title** to get an idea of what the diagram is about.

B Study the **images** closely to understand each part of the diagram.

C Look at the **captions** and the **labels** for more information.

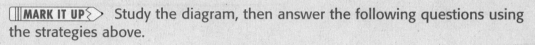

MARK IT UP Study the diagram, then answer the following questions using the strategies above.

1. What does this diagram show? _____

_____

2. What is one structural difference between the seismograph that records side-to-side motion and the one that records up-and-down motion?

_____

3. Circle the arrows that show which way the drums are rotating.

4. Why do you think the pen in the seismograph that measures up-and-down motion is held by a spring?

_____

Seismographs

An instrument called a **seismograph** detects and records waves produced by earthquakes that may have originated hundreds, and even thousands, of kilometers away. Because earthquakes produce different types of wave motions, there are different types of seismographs.

Seismograph A

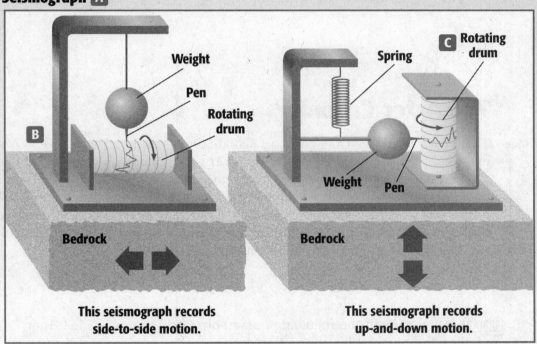

Weight
Pen
Rotating drum
B
Bedrock

This seismograph records side-to-side motion.

Spring
C Rotating drum
Weight
Pen
Bedrock

This seismograph records up-and-down motion.

Main Idea and Supporting Details

The *main idea* in a paragraph is its most important point. *Details* in the paragraph support the main idea. Identifying the main idea will help you focus on the main message the writer wants to communicate. Use the following strategies to help you identify a paragraph's main idea and supporting details.

- Look for the **main idea,** which is often the first sentence in a paragraph.

- Use the main idea to help you **summarize** the point of the paragraph.

- Identify specific **details,** including facts and examples, that **support** the main idea.

The Aztec Calendar

Main idea The Aztecs used two calendars to calculate time—a solar calendar of 365 days and a religious or ritual one of 260 days. The two calendars were round and meshed like gears. Once every 52 years, the calendars would start on the same day. This important event was marked with a special ritual called Binding Up of the Years, or the New Fire Ceremony. As the day approached, all fires were left to burn out. During the ceremony, a priest kindled a new fire that would be used to light all the fires of the community.

Details

[||MARK IT UP] Read the following paragraph. Circle the main idea. Then underline the paragraph's supporting details.

In 1790, a circular Aztec calendar stone was discovered in Mexico City. The stone is about 13 feet in diameter and weighs 24 tons. In the center is the sun god, Tonatiuh. He is surrounded by four panels that represent the four previous ages of the earth. Arrayed around these are 20 segments representing the 20 days of each of the 18 Aztec months, totaling 360 days. The five extra days were considered to be unlucky.

Problem and Solution

Does the proposed solution to a problem make sense? In order to decide, you need to look at each part of the text. Use the following strategies to read the text below.

- Look at the beginning or middle of a paragraph to find the **statement of the problem.**
- Find **details** that explain the problem and tell why it is important.
- Look for the **proposed solution.**
- Identify the **supporting details** for the proposed solution.
- Think about whether the solution is a good one.

A Stoplight Can Prevent Accidents

by Manuel Marcus

Statement of a problem

It happened again last night. Two cars collided at the intersection of West Ave. and Beach St. This is the sixth accident that has taken place at that intersection in the past year. Luckily, no one has been seriously injured or killed so far. But we need to do something before it's too late.

Explanation of problem

This intersection is so dangerous because West Ave. bends around just before the corner of Beach St. This means that drivers or cyclists aren't able to see cars approaching on West Ave. until they're entering the intersection. They have to just take their chances and hope they make it to the other side. Too many don't.

One action that would help eliminate this problem would be to put a stoplight at the intersection. This would allow drivers to proceed safely across in both directions. It would also slow traffic down and force people to pay more attention to their driving. Although it would cost the community some money, think how much it would save in car repairs, personal injuries, and possibly, even lives.

Here's what you can do to help support this solution:
- Stop procrastinating.
- Look at the facts.
- Go to the village hall and sign a petition.

MARK IT UP Use the text and strategies above to answer these questions.

1. Underline the proposed solution.

2. Circle at least one reason that supports this solution.

3. Explain why you think this is or is not a good solution to the problem.

Sequence

It's important to understand the *sequence, or order of events,* in what you read. This helps you understand what happens and why. The tips below can help you understand sequence in any type of text.

- Read through a passage, looking for the **main steps** or stages.

- Look for **words and phrases that signal time,** such as *around 3000 B.C., from 900 B.C. to 200 B.C.,* and *several years later.*

- Look for **words and phrases that signal order,** such as *meanwhile, before that,* and *finally.*

|||MARK IT UP⟩ Read the passage about Andean cultures on the next page. Then use the information from the article and the tips above to answer the questions.

1. Underline the words or phrases that signal time.

2. Circle the words or phrases that signal order.

3. A time line can help you understand the sequence of events. Use the information from the article to complete this time line.

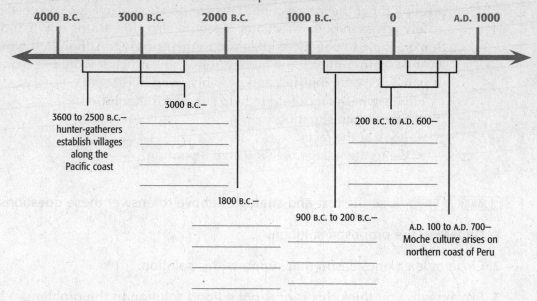

| 4000 B.C. | 3000 B.C. | 2000 B.C. | 1000 B.C. | 0 | A.D. 1000 |

3000 B.C.—

3600 to 2500 B.C.—
hunter-gatherers
establish villages
along the
Pacific coast

200 B.C. to A.D. 600—

1800 B.C.—

900 B.C. to 200 B.C.—

A.D. 100 to A.D. 700—
Moche culture arises on
northern coast of Peru

Societies Grow in the Andes Regions

South America's first advanced civilizations emerged in the northern Andes region, in what is now Peru—a difficult place to launch a culture. The terrain is steep and rocky, and the climate is severe. Between the mountains and the Pacific Ocean lies a narrow plain crossed in some places by rivers. It was in these river valleys that the first settlements occurred.

Between 3600 and 2500 B.C., people began to establish temporary villages along the Pacific coast. These first inhabitants were hunter-gatherers who relied on seafood and small game for their survival. Eventually, around 3000 B.C., these people began to farm. By 1800 B.C., a number of thriving communities existed along the coast.

The first influential civilization arose not on the coast, however, but in the mountains. This culture, known as the Chavín, flourished from 900 B.C. to 200 B.C. Its influence spread quickly across most of northern and central Peru. Because archaeologists have found no evidence of political or economic organization, they conclude that the Chavín was primarily a religious civilization. Like the Olmec in Mesoamerica, the Chavín may have acted as a "mother culture."

Around the time Chavín culture declined, other civilizations were emerging in Peru. The Nazca culture flourished along the southern coast of Peru from around 200 B.C. to A.D. 600. In this extremely dry area, the Nazca developed extensive irrigation systems and beautiful textiles and pottery. They also created the Nazca lines, huge drawings of animals and plants that can only be seen from the air.

Meanwhile, on the northern coast of Peru, another civilization was reaching great heights. This was the Moche culture, which lasted from about A.D. 100 to A.D. 700. The Moche took advantage of the rivers that flowed from the Andes, building impressive systems to irrigate their varied crops. This was a wealthy civilization, judging by the many articles of gold, silver, and precious stones and exquisite ceramics it left behind.

Cause and Effect

A *cause* is an event that brings about another event. An *effect* is something that happens as a result of the first event. Identifying causes and effects helps you understand how events are related. Use the tips below to find causes and effects in any kind of reading.

- Look for an action or event that answers the question, "What happened?" This is the **effect.**

- Look for an action or event that answers the question, "Why did this happen?" This is the **cause.**

- Look for words or phrases that signal causes and effects, such as *because, as a result, therefore, consequently,* and *since.*

MARK IT UP Read the cause-and-effect passage on the next page. Then use the strategies above to help you answer the following questions.

1. Circle words in the passage that signal causes and effects. The first one has been done for you.

2. What two causes are given for cutting down trees in the rain forest?

   _____

   _____

3. Causes often have multiple effects. Complete the following diagram showing the effects of destruction of the rain forests.

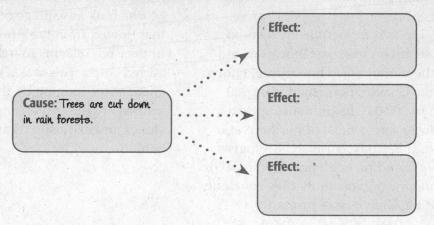

Cause: Trees are cut down in rain forests.

Effect:

Effect:

Effect:

We're Destroying Our Rain Forests

Effect Imagine a lush, green place that is home to over half of all the animal and plant species on Earth. You don't really have to imagine very hard, because that place—the rain forest—actually exists. The largest rain forest, in the Amazon River basin, covers about 2 million square miles of Brazil, Ecuador, and Peru. Unfortunately, rain forests like this one are being destroyed at an increasingly alarming rate.

According to a study done by U.S. and Brazilian scientists, nearly 5 million acres of this rain forest are disappearing a year. That's equal to seven football fields a minute.

Cause The cause of this destruction is simple—cutting down trees. Every minute, around 2,000 trees are felled to create highways, railroads, and farms. Some trees, such as mahogany and teak, are harvested for their beautiful hardwood.

This destruction of the rain forests has wide-ranging effects. Tens of thousands of plants and animals call the rain forests home—about 30,000 plant species in the Amazon rain forest alone. In addition to important food products such as bananas, coffee, nuts, and chocolate, these plants include medicinal compounds found nowhere else on Earth. As for animals, scientists estimate that an area of just 4 square miles of a rain forest shelters more than 550 species of birds, reptiles, and amphibians. Because their habitat is disappearing, almost 100 species face extinction every day.

Rain forests also act as climate regulators. They balance the exchange of water and carbon dioxide in the atmosphere and help offset global warming. The Earth's well-being will suffer increasingly as a result of the rain forests' destruction.

If this process is not reversed, it may be over within 50 years. The teeming, thriving rain forest will be a thing of the past.

Comparison and Contrast

Comparing two things means showing how they are the same. *Contrasting* two things means showing how they are different. Comparisons and contrasts are often used in science and history books to make a subject clearer. Use these tips to help you understand comparison and contrast in reading assignments such as the article on the opposite page.

- Look for **direct statements** of comparison and contrast. "These things are similar because…" or "One major difference is…"

- Pay attention to **words and phrases that signal comparisons,** such as *also, both, is the same as,* and *in the same way.*

- Notice **words and phrases that signal contrasts.** Some of these are *however, still, but,* and *in contrast.*

MARK IT UP Read the article on the next page. Then use the information from the article and the tips above to answer the questions.

1. Circle the words and phrases that signal comparisons. A sample has been done for you.

2. Underline the words and phrases that signal contrasts. Notice the completed sample.

3. A Venn diagram shows how two subjects are similar and how they are different. Complete this diagram, which uses information from the article to compare and contrast yerba maté and green tea. Add one or more similarities to the center of the diagram and one or more differences to each outer circle.

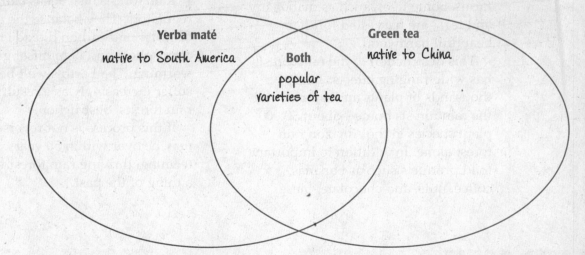

Yerba maté
native to South America

Both
popular
varieties of tea

Green tea
native to China

Two for Tea: Yerba Maté and Green Tea

Next to water, tea is the most popular drink all over the world. Served hot or iced, it comes in a variety to suit any taste. (Both) yerba maté and green tea are varieties that seem to suit the tastes of an increasing number of people all over the world.

Yerba maté is native to South America. It is made from the dried leaves of the yerba maté tree, an evergreen whose scientific name is *Ilex paraguariensis*. Green tea, on the other hand, is native to China and was exported to Japan in about A.D. 800. Its leaves, like the leaves of black tea, come from the *Camellia sinensis* plant.

Another difference between yerba maté and green tea is the way the beverage is brewed. In South America, yerba maté is traditionally brewed in hollow gourds, themselves called matés. The gourd is filled three-quarters full with leaves, which are then covered with boiling water. When that has been completely absorbed, more water is added. The brewed tea is then drunk through a tube with a strainer at one end, called a bombilla. Maté is often served with milk, sugar, or lemon juice to cut its slight bitterness.

Green tea, however, usually is brewed in teapots. Only about a teaspoon of leaves is used per pot. The leaves are steeped for only two minutes or so—much less time than the repeated soaking for yerba maté. Green tea has a mild taste and is served plain in ceramic cups.

No matter how they are brewed and drunk, though, both yerba maté and green tea are thought to offer many health benefits. Each is loaded with antioxidants that may boost the immune system and help prevent cancer. Yerba maté is thought to aid digestion. Similarly, green tea has been reputed to lower cholesterol and blood sugar and relieve the pain of arthritis.

So, no matter which tea you choose—yerba maté or green tea—here's to your health and good taste!

Persuasion

Persuasion is giving an opinion backed up with reasons and facts. Examining an opinion and the reasons and facts that support it will help you decide if the opinion makes sense. Look at the persuasive essay on the next page as you read these tips.

- Look for words or phrases that **signal an opinion,** such as *I believe, I think,* and *in my opinion.*

- Identify reasons, facts, or expert opinions that **support** the writer's position.

- Ask yourself if the writer's position and the reasons that back it up **make sense.**

- Look for **errors in reasoning,** such as overgeneralizations, that may affect the persuasiveness of the writer.

[||MARK IT UP⟩⟩ Read the persuasive essay on the following page. Then use the strategies above to help you answer the following questions.

1. Circle any words or phrases that signal an opinion.

2. Underline any words or phrases that signal the writer's opinion.

3. The writer presents both sides of this issue. List the points supporting both sides in the chart below.

Tape recorders should be allowed	Tape recorders should not be allowed
Tape recorders can be an aid to learning.	

THIS SHOULD BE TAPE-RECORDED

The school board of District 163 just passed a policy banning personal tape recorders in the schools. I disagree with this decision and believe not only that tape recorders should be allowed, but also that they can be an aid to learning.

In a public meeting held to discuss this issue, most people supported the policy for two reasons. Some thought that tape recorders would distract students from their school activities. Others believed that they would tempt students to cut classes. Students would just assign one person to tape-record the lesson and make copies of the tape for everyone else.

In my opinion, neither of these reasons is valid. None of my teachers would ever allow a student to listen to a tape recorder or a CD player during class. In addition, attendance is a significant part of every student's grade, and most wouldn't risk cutting class, even if someone offered to tape it for them. Besides, listening to a tape would take just as long as sitting through the class itself.

More important, though, are the ways tape recorders can enhance learning. The first is that tapes can supplement students' notes. Everyone's mind drifts off sometimes, and having a tape of the lesson could

help students fill in gaps and clarify confusing points.

The most important role for tape recorders, however, is in language classes. In other academic areas, students just have to learn specific information. In language classes, however, they also have to remember how words should sound when they're spoken. If students were allowed to tape their language lessons, they could use the tape to help improve their speaking skills and supplement the meager hour a week they have in the language lab.

In summary, I think that the policy banning tape recorders in the schools should be repealed. Students are mature enough to use recording technology to improve, not impede, their academic success. And I believe they should be given the chance.

Social Studies

Social studies class becomes easier when you understand how your textbook's words, pictures, and maps work together to give you information. Following these tips can make you a better reader of social studies lessons. As you read the tips, look at the sample lesson on the right-hand page.

A Read the **headline** and **subheads** of the lesson. These give you an idea what the section covers.

B Make sure you know the meaning of any boldfaced or underlined **vocabulary items.** These terms often appear on tests.

C Think about **how information is organized**. Social studies books often present ideas using sequence, cause and effect, comparison and contrast, and main idea and supporting details.

D Look closely at **graphics** such as maps and illustrations. Think about what information these features add to the text.

E Notice text that is set off in some way on the page, such as in a tinted box. This material may give **firsthand information** about a topic.

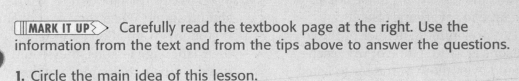

MARK IT UP Carefully read the textbook page at the right. Use the information from the text and from the tips above to answer the questions.

1. Circle the main idea of this lesson.

2. Draw a box around one vocabulary term defined on this page.

3. How is the information about the Spanish colonies in the Americas presented—by cause and effect or by sequence?

_____

4. What details do the quotation in the tint box and the illustration provide about Spanish rule in the Americas?

_____

_____

The Spanish and Native Americans

A

TERMS & NAMES
viceroyalty
encomienda
hacienda
mission
Popé
plantation
Bartolomé de Las Casas
Columbian Exchange

C **MAIN IDEA**

Spanish rule in the Americas had terrible consequences for Native Americans.

WHY IT MATTERS NOW

The destruction of Native American cultures created social problems that continue today.

ONE AMERICAN'S STORY

Huamán Poma, a Peruvian Native American, was angry about the abuse the Spanish heaped upon Native Americans. He wrote to King Philip III of Spain to complain about the bad treatment.

E *A VOICE FROM THE PAST*

It is their [the Spanish] practice to collect Indians into groups and send them to forced labor without wages, while they themselves receive the payment for the work. . . . The royal administrators and the other Spaniards lord it over the Indians with absolute power.

Huamán Poma, *Letter to a King*

In his letter, Poma asked the king to help the Native Americans and uphold the rule of law in Peru. If the king actually read the letter, it made no difference. Spanish colonists continued to mistreat Native Americans as the Spanish Empire expanded in the Americas.

D

A Spanish priest forces a Native American woman to work at a loom.

A Spanish Colonies in the Americas

The Spanish Empire grew rapidly, despite efforts by other European countries to compete with Spain. By 1700, it controlled much of the Americas. Spain took several steps to establish an effective colonial government. First, it divided its American empire into two provinces called B New Spain and Peru. Each province was called a **viceroyalty**. The top official of each viceroyalty was called the viceroy. He ruled in the king's name.

The Spanish also built new roads to transport people and goods across the empire. These roads stretched outward from the capitals at Mexico City and Lima. The roads helped Spain to control the colonies by allowing soldiers to move quickly from place to place. Roads also improved the Spanish economy because materials, such as gold and silver, could be transported efficiently to the coast and then to Spain.

European Exploration of the Americas **71**

Reading a science textbook becomes easier when you understand how the explanations, drawings, and special terms work together. Use the strategies below to help you better understand your science textbook. Look at the examples on the opposite page as you read each strategy in this list.

A Preview the **title** and any **headings** to see what scientific concepts will be covered.

B Read the **key ideas, objectives,** or **focus.** These items summarize the lesson and establish a purpose for your reading.

C Look for **boldfaced** and **italicized** terms that appear in the text. Look for the definitions of these terms.

D Carefully examine any **pictures** or **diagrams.** Read the **captions** and evaluate how the graphics help illustrate and explain the text.

MARK IT UP Use the sample science lesson and the strategies above to answer the following questions.

1. What are the two main ideas that will be covered in this lesson?

_____

_____

2. Underline the definition of an ocean current.

3. What direction do ocean currents turn in the Northern Hemisphere?

_____

4. Which other chapter of the book might you need to read to better understand this lesson?

_____

5. Based on the illustration, where do most of the cool currents flow?

_____

24.1

B KEY IDEAS

Surface currents are driven primarily by the wind.

There are several types of surface currents.

KEY VOCABULARY
• ocean current
• surface current
• cold-core ring
• warm-core ring
• countercurrent

VISUALIZATIONS
CLASSZONE.COM

Examine global surface currents.
Keycode: ES2401

A Surface Currents

The water in the oceans is constantly on the move. Some motions, such as waves, are obvious. Other types of motion are so subtle or so deep that they are barely noticeable. These movements, called ocean currents, usually involve large water masses. An **ocean current** is any continuous flow of water along a broad path in the ocean. Ocean currents may flow at the surface or far below it.

C A **surface current** is an ocean current that generally flows in the upper 1000 meters of the ocean. Surface currents are primarily driven by the wind. The Global Ocean Currents map below shows surface currents of the world. You can make several observations from the map. First, the Atlantic Ocean and the Pacific Ocean each have two circles of ocean currents, one in the Northern Hemisphere and another in the Southern Hemisphere. Consider as well that the direction in which each current circulates depends on the Coriolis Effect (Chapter 19): hence ocean currents in the Northern Hemisphere turn clockwise, and in the Southern Hemisphere, counterclockwise. As you see, the circular currents of the North Atlantic and North Pacific turn clockwise, while the currents of the South Atlantic and South Pacific turn counterclockwise.

You can also see from this map that the temperature of the currents follows a pattern. Currents flowing away from the equator carry warm water. Currents flowing toward the equator carry cold water. This occurs because areas near the equator have warmer temperatures and areas near the poles have colder temperatures.

D **Global Ocean Currents**

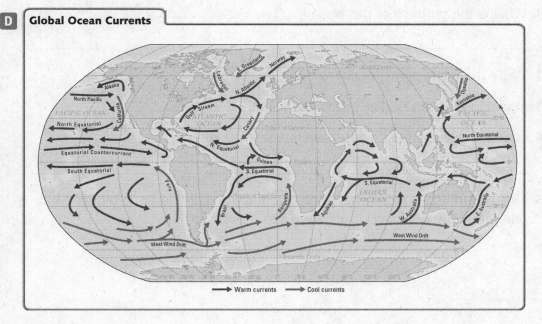

→ Warm currents → Cool currents

Mathematics

Reading in mathematics is different from reading in history, literature, or science. Use the following strategies to help you better understand your math textbook. Look at the example on the next page as you read each strategy.

A Preview the **title** and **headings** to see which math concepts will be covered or reviewed.

B Find and read the **goals** or **instructions** for completing the lesson. These will tell you the most important points to know and how to proceed.

C Identify **vocabulary** and **concepts** you will be responsible for understanding and applying.

D Study any **worked-out solutions** to sample problems. These are the key to understanding how to complete the exercises.

||||MARK IT UP⟩ Use the strategies above and the mathematics lesson on the next page to answer the following questions.

1. What is the purpose of this lesson? _____

_____

2. Circle the instructions for completing the lesson.

3. Underline the vocabulary terms you will need to define.

4. How many exercises do you have to complete in item 9.5?

_____

5. This lesson lists a page where you can find the definition of a tangent and later gives the definition itself. Put a box around each.

Notebook Review

Check Your Definitions

trigonometric ratio, p. 463   cosine, p. 463

sine, p. 463   tangent, p. 463

C

Use Your Vocabulary

1. Copy and complete: To write the sine ratio for a given acute angle of a right triangle, you need to know the length of the side ? the angle and the length of the ? .

9.5 Can you find side lengths of special right triangles?

Review **EXAMPLE** Find the length of the hypotenuse. Give the exact answer.

hypotenuse = leg · $\sqrt{2}$ **Rule for 45°-45°-90° triangle**

        = $26\sqrt{2}$ **Substitute.**

ANSWER The length of the hypotenuse is $26\sqrt{2}$ feet.

☑ **Find the value of each variable. Give the exact answer.**

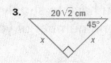

2.   **3.** 20$\sqrt{2}$ cm   **4.**

9.6 Can you use trigonometric ratios?

Review **EXAMPLE** In △ABC, write the sine, cosine, and tangent ratios for ∠A. **D**

$\sin A = \dfrac{\text{opposite}}{\text{hypotenuse}} = \dfrac{12}{37}$

$\cos A = \dfrac{\text{adjacent}}{\text{hypotenuse}} = \dfrac{35}{37}$

$\tan A = \dfrac{\text{opposite}}{\text{adjacent}} = \dfrac{12}{35}$

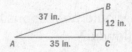

Reading an Application

Reading and understanding an application will help you fill it out correctly and avoid mistakes. Use the following strategies to understand any application. Refer to the example on the next page as you read each strategy.

A **Begin at the top.** Scan the application to understand the different sections.

B Look for special **warnings, conditions,** or **instructions for filling out** the application.

C Note any **references** that must be included with the application.

D Pay attention to **optional sections,** or **questions you don't have to answer.**

E Look for difficult or confusing words or abbreviations. Look them up in a dictionary or ask someone what they mean.

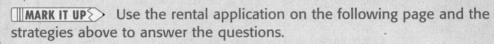 **MARK IT UP** Use the rental application on the following page and the strategies above to answer the questions.

1. Circle the part of the application that asks about your bank accounts.

2. What information do you have to supply about your current job besides name, address, and phone number of your employer?

   _____

3. When is rent due?

   _____

4. Who would be responsible for the damage caused if your bathtub overflowed?

   _____

5. **ASSESSMENT PRACTICE** Circle the letter of the correct answer.
   If you are renting an apartment with a roommate, your roommate should

   A. sign the bottom of your application next to your name.

   B. fill out a separate application.

   C. complete the information for Personal Reference.

   D. make a copy of your application and sign it.

A Apartment Rental Application

NAME OF APPLICANT   HOME PHONE NUMBER   DATE

PRESENT ADDRESS

PRESENT LANDLORD   ADDRESS   PHONE NUMBER

CURRENT EMPLOYER   ADDRESS   PHONE NUMBER

POSITION   TYPE OF BUSINESS   SALARY   LENGTH OF EMPLOYMENT

PERSONAL REFERENCE (NAME) C   ADDRESS   PHONE NUMBER

EMERGENCY CONTACT (NAME)   ADDRESS   PHONE NUMBER

BANK-CHECKING ACCOUNT   ACCOUNT NUMBER

BANK-SAVINGS ACCOUNT   ACCOUNT NUMBER

NAMES OF ALL CO-TENANTS (EACH ADULT MUST COMPLETE A SEPARATE APPLICATION) D

APARTMENT NO./TYPE   TOTAL NO. OF OCCUPANTS   RENT PER MONTH $

ADDRESS

LEASE TERM (MONTHS)   FROM (DATE)   TO (DATE)

Rent is due on the first day of each month in advance.
The applicant authorizes the renting agency to obtain a consumer credit report for the applicant. B
The owner and the management are not responsible for the loss of personal belongings caused by fire, theft, smoke, water or otherwise, unless caused by their negligence. E

Signature_____

Reading a Public Notice

Public notices can tell you about events in your community and give you valuable information about safety. When you read a public notice, follow these tips. Each tip relates to a specific part of the notice on the next page.

A Read the notice's **title,** if it has one. The title often gives the main idea or purpose of the notice.

B Pay attention to information presented in **different typefaces,** such as boldface or underline. This often indicates main topics or subtopics.

C Look for **details** about where and when events will take place.

D Look for **descriptions** of individual events.

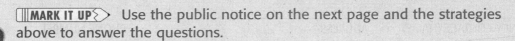

MARK IT UP Use the public notice on the next page and the strategies above to answer the questions.

1. What is the purpose of this notice?

_____

2. Circle the date and time of the meeting of the Committee to Restore George Washington's Portrait.

3. Put a star next to the meetings that will NOT be held at the Town Hall.

4. If you are interested in the proposed smoking ban, what meeting should you attend?

_____

5. **ASSESSMENT PRACTICE** Circle the letter of the correct answer.
   When will permits for house additions be discussed?
   A. Thursday, August 7, 7:00 P.M.
   B. Monday, August 11, 7:00 P.M.
   C. Wednesday, August 20, 4:00 P.M.
   D. Thursday, August 21, 7:00 P.M.

Meetings A

Planning Board:
  Tuesday, Aug. 5, 7 P.M., Town Hall.
Committee to Restore George Washington's Portrait: B
  Wednesday, Aug. 6, 5 P.M., Town Hall.
Grant Committee:
  Wednesday, Aug. 6, 7 P.M., Town Hall. C
Conservation Commission:
  Thursday, Aug. 7, 7 P.M., Town Hall.
  Agenda (specific times for individual hearings not given):
  Public Hearing concerning a Request for Amendment to the Order of
  Conditions issued to the Department of Public Works for sewer and storm
  drain replacement;
  B Public Hearing concerning a Request for Determination for a proposed
  roof to be installed over an existing open deck;
  D Public Hearing concerning a Stormwater Permit Application in conjunction
  with construction of a two-story addition on Adams Street;
  Public Hearing concerning a Stormwater Permit Application in conjunction
  with construction of a two-story addition on Kimball Road.
Board of Health:
  Monday, Aug. 11, 6 P.M., Town Hall. Agenda: Consideration of and vote on
  proposed smoking ban.
Building, Planning, and Construction Committee:
  Monday, Aug. 11, 7 P.M., Endicott Estate.
Finance Committee:
  Thursday, Aug. 14, 7 P.M., Town Hall.
Board of Assessors:
  Wednesday, Aug. 20, 4 P.M., Town Hall.
School Committee:
  Wednesday, Aug. 20, 7 P.M., School Administration Building.
Board of Selectmen:
  Thursday, Aug. 21, 7 P.M., Town Hall.
Conservation Commission:
  Thursday, Aug. 21, 7 P.M., Town Hall.
Library Trustees:
  Tuesday, Aug. 26, 7 P.M., Endicott Branch Library.

Reading a Web Page

When you research information for a report or project, you may use the World Wide Web. Once you find the site you want, the strategies below will help you find the facts and details you need. Look at the sample Web page on the right as you read each of the strategies.

A Notice the page's **Web address,** or URL. You may want to write it down or bookmark it if you think you might access the page at another time.

B Look for **menu bars** along the top, bottom, or side of the page. These guide you to other parts of the site that may be useful.

C Look for **links** to other parts of the site or to related pages. Links are often highlighted in color or underlined.

D Use a search **feature** to quickly find out whether the information you want to locate appears anywhere on the site.

MARK IT UP Read the Web site on the opposite page. Then use the information from the site and the tips above to answer the questions.

1. Circle the Web address of this site.

2. Which menu option would you click to view comments from other visitors to the site?

_____

3. Put a star by the link that includes information about job openings for Latinos.

4. Draw a box around the links you would click to get information about the Crisis in Education.

5. **ASSESSMENT PRACTICE** Circle the letter of the correct answer.
   What is Learning Crisis?
   A. a chatroom
   B. a Web page for teachers
   C. a feature article
   D. the English translation of a Spanish Web site

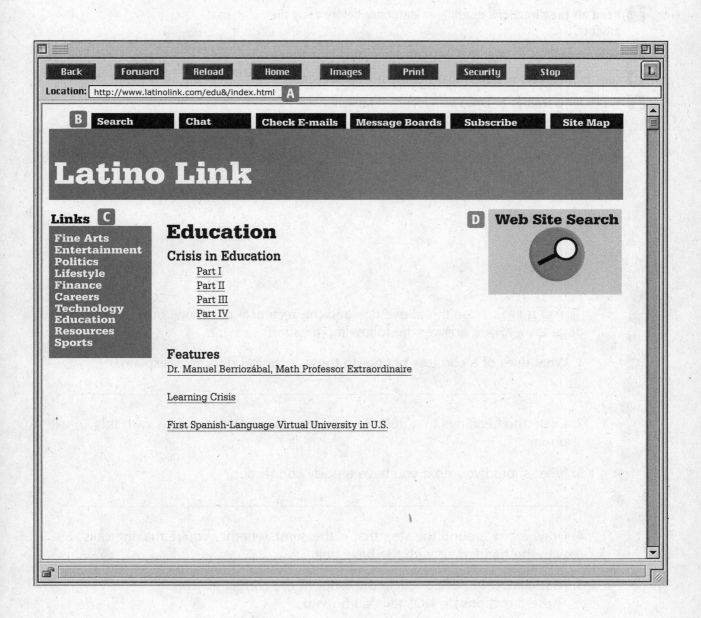

Back | **Forward** | **Reload** | **Home** | **Images** | **Print** | **Security** | **Stop** L

Location: http://www.latinolink.com/edu&/index.html A

B **Search** | **Chat** | **Check E-mails** | **Message Boards** | **Subscribe** | **Site Map**

Latino Link

Links C

Fine Arts
Entertainment
Politics
Lifestyle
Finance
Careers
Technology
Education
Resources
Sports

Education

Crisis in Education

Part I
Part II
Part III
Part IV

Features

Dr. Manuel Berriozábal, Math Professor Extraordinaire

Learning Crisis

First Spanish-Language Virtual University in U.S.

D **Web Site Search**

Reading Technical Directions

Reading technical directions will help you understand how to use the products you buy. Use the following tips to help you read a variety of technical directions.

A Look carefully at any **diagrams** or **other images** of the product.

B **Read all the directions** carefully at least once before using the product.

C Notice **headings** or **lines** that separate one section from another.

D Look for **numbers** or **letters** that give the steps in sequence.

E Watch for **warnings** or **notes** with more information.

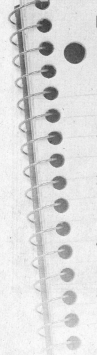

MARK IT UP Use the above tips and the technical directions on the next page to help you answer the following questions.

1. What uses of a cordless phone do these technical directions explain?

   _____

2. Circle the headings that describe two ways you can make calls with this phone.

3. What should you do if you have a noisy connection?

   _____

4. Draw a box around the step that is the same whether you're making calls with the handset or with the base unit.

5. **ASSESSMENT PRACTICE** Circle the letter of the correct answer.
   These directions do NOT tell you how to
   A. switch a call with the handset to the speakerphone.
   B. hang up using the handset and the base unit.
   C. answer a call with the handset off the base unit.
   D. make a call using the speed dial feature.

Using a Cordless Phone

Making Calls

With the Handset

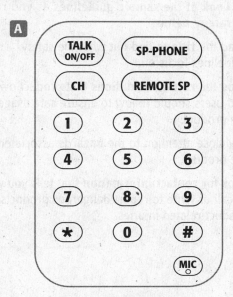

B 1 Press `TALK ON/OFF`.

2 Dial a phone number.

3 To hang up, press `TALK ON/OFF` or put the handset on the base unit.

• If noise is interfering with your conversation, press `CH` to choose a clearer channel or move closer to the base unit.

• To switch a call to the speakerphone, press `REMOTE SP`. To hang up, press `SP-PHONE` or `REMOTE SP`.

• Like a standard phone, you can dial with the base unit keypad after pressing `TALK ON/OFF`.

With the Base Unit

D 1 Press `SP-PHONE`.

2 Dial a phone number.

3 Speak into the `MIC`. To hang up, press `SP-PHONE`.

Answering Call **C**

With the Handset

If the handset is off the base unit, press `TALK ON/OFF`. OR If the handset is on the base unit, just lift up.

With the Base Unit

Press `SP-PHONE`, then speak into the `MIC`.

• If the handset is off the base unit, you can also answer the call by pressing any dial button (0 to 9, ∗, or #). **E**

Reading Product Information: Safety Guidelines

Safety guidelines are facts and recommendations provided by government agencies or product manufacturers offering instructions and warnings about safe use of their products. Learning to read and follow such guidelines is important for your safety. Look at the sample guidelines as you read each strategy below.

A Read the **title** to find out what the safety guidelines focus on.

B Read the **recommendations** that product owners and users should follow to ensure safe usage of the product.

C Pay close attention to the **hazards** associated with the product.

D Look for **contact information** that tells you where to call or write to report dangerous products or product-related injuries.

A **SAFEGUARDS FOR USING YOUR FOOD PROCESSOR**

When using electrical appliances, these basic safety precautions should always be followed:

- Read all instructions carefully before use. **B**
- To protect against electric shock, do not put the base of the appliance in water or any other liquid.
- Close supervision is necessary when the appliance is used by or near children.
- Unplug from the outlet when not in use, before putting on or taking off parts, and before cleaning.
- Avoid contact with moving parts of the appliance.
- Do not operate any appliance with a damaged cord or plug or after the appliance malfunctions, or is dropped or damaged in any manner. Return the appliance to nearest authorized Consumer Service Center for examination, repair, or adjustment. **C**
- The use of attachments not recommended or sold by the manufacturer may cause fire, electric shock, or injury.
- Do not use the appliance outdoors.
- Do not let the cord hang over the edge of a table or counter, or touch hot surfaces.

To report a defective or dangerous product, call (800) 555-5377. D

MARK IT UP Use the safety guidelines to help you answer the following questions.

1. Underline the precaution you should take when the food processor is running.

2. What should you do with a damaged appliance?

3. Put a box around the step to take before cleaning the food processor.

4. **ASSESSMENT PRACTICE** Circle the letter of the correct answer.
   In which situation can the food processor be safely operated?
   A. outdoors
   B. using recommended attachments
   C. in the sink
   D. on a hot stove

Reading a Museum Schedule

Knowing how to read a museum schedule accurately can help you plan your visit. Look at the example as you read each strategy on this list.

A Look at the **title** to know what the schedule covers.

B Identify **labels** that show dates or **days of the week** to help you understand how the daily or weekly schedule works.

C Look for **expressions of time** to know what hours or minutes are listed on the schedule.

D Look for **changes** or **exceptions** to the regular schedule.

Museum of Science and Industry

Summer Hours (June 14–Labor Day)

Daily: 9:30 A.M.–7:00 P.M. **C**

Discovery Space: 9:30 A.M.–6:00 P.M.
(special area for children 6 and under)

Notes: Hands-on Labs are usually open from 10:00 A.M.–5:30 P.M. during the summer. These hours, however, are subject to change. Call ahead. **D**

Submarine Summer Tour Hours

Regular Tour Daily: 10:00 A.M.–5:30 P.M. $5.00

Tech Tour **B** First Sunday of each month $15.00 (Call for schedule)

Please note that you must be at least 3 years old to tour the sub. **D**

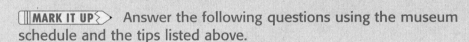

MARK IT UP Answer the following questions using the museum schedule and the tips listed above.

1. Circle the museum's regular hours.

2. Who is not allowed to tour the submarine?

_____

3. When does the Discovery Space close?

_____

4. **ASSESSMENT PRACTICE** Circle the letter of the correct answer.
   What should you do if you want to visit the Hands-on Labs?
   A. Plan to go on the first Sunday of the month.
   B. Bring a child over the age of six with you.
   C. Check to see what hours it is open.
   D. Make arrangements by calling 503.555.4624.

Test Preparation Strategies

In this section you'll find strategies and practice to help you with many different kinds of standardized tests. The strategies apply to questions based on long and short readings, as well as questions about charts, graphs, and product labels. You'll also find examples and practice for revising-and-editing tests and writing tests. Applying the strategies to the practice materials and thinking through the answers will help you succeed in many formal testing situations.

Test Preparation Strategies

You can prepare for tests in several ways. First, study and understand the content that will be on the test. Second, learn as many test-taking techniques as you can. These techniques will help you better understand the questions and how to answer them. Following are some general suggestions for preparing for and taking tests. Starting on page 184, you'll find more detailed suggestions and test-taking practice.

Successful Test Taking

 Study Content Throughout the Year

1. **Master the content of your class.** The best way to study for tests is to read, understand, and review the content of your class. Read your daily assignments carefully. Study the notes that you have taken in class. Participate in class discussions. Work with classmates in small groups to help one another learn. You might trade writing assignments and comment on your classmates' work.

2. **Use your textbook for practice.** Your textbook includes many different types of questions. Some may ask you to talk about a story you just read. Others may ask you to figure out what's wrong with a sentence or how to make a paragraph sound better. Try answering these questions out loud and in writing. This type of practice can make taking a test much easier.

3. **Learn how to understand the information in charts, maps, and graphic organizers.** One type of test question may ask you to look at a graphic organizer, such as a spider map, and explain something about the information you see there. Another type of question may ask you to look at a map to find a particular place. You'll find charts, maps, and graphic organizers to study in your textbook. You'll also find charts, maps, and graphs in your science, mathematics, literature, and social studies textbooks. When you look at these, ask yourself, What information is being presented and why is it important?

4. **Practice taking tests.** Use copies of tests you have taken in the past or in other classes for practice. Every test has a time limit, so set a timer for 15 or 20 minutes and then begin your practice. Try to finish the test in the time you've given yourself.

☑ **Reading Check** In what practical way can your textbook help you prepare for a test?

5. Talk about test-taking experiences. After you've taken a classroom test or quiz, talk about it with your teacher and classmates. Which types of questions were the hardest to understand? What made them difficult? Which questions seemed easiest, and why? When you share test-taking techniques with your classmates, everyone can become a successful test taker.

Use Strategies During the Test

1. Read the directions carefully. You can't be a successful test taker unless you know exactly what you are expected to do. Look for key words and phrases, such as *circle the best answer, write a paragraph,* or *choose the word that best completes each sentence.*

2. Learn how to read test questions. Test questions can sometimes be difficult to figure out. They may include unfamiliar language or be written in an unfamiliar way. Try rephrasing the question in a simpler way using words you understand. Always ask yourself, What type of information does this question want me to provide?

3. Pay special attention when using a separate answer sheet. If you accidentally skip a line on an answer sheet, all the rest of your answers may be wrong! Try one or more of the following techniques:

- Use a ruler on the answer sheet to make sure you are placing your answers on the correct line.

- After every five answers, check to make sure you're on the right line.

- Each time you turn a page of the test booklet, check to make sure the number of the question is the same as the number of the answer line on the answer sheet.

- If the answer sheet has circles, fill them in neatly. A stray pencil mark might cause the scoring machine to count the answer as incorrect.

4. If you're not sure of the answer, make your best guess. Unless you've been told that there is a penalty for guessing, choose the answer that you think is likeliest to be correct.

5. Keep track of the time. Answering all the questions on a test usually results in a better score. That's why finishing the test is important. Keep track of the time you have left. At the beginning of the test, figure out how many questions you will have to answer by the halfway point in order to finish in the time given.

☑ **Reading Check** What are at least two good ways to avoid skipping lines on an answer sheet?

Understand Types of Test Questions

Most tests include two types of questions: multiple choice and open-ended. Specific strategies will help you understand and correctly answer each type of question.

A **multiple-choice question** has two parts. The first part is the question itself, called the stem. The second part is a series of possible answers. Usually four possible answers are provided, and only one of them is correct. Your task is to choose the correct answer. Here are some strategies to help you do just that.

1. Read and think about each question carefully before looking at the possible answers.

2. Pay close attention to key words in the question. For example, look for the word *not*, as in "Which of the following is not a cause of the conflict in this story?"

3. Read and think about all of the possible answers before making your choice.

4. Reduce the number of choices by eliminating any answers you know are incorrect. Then, think about why some of the remaining choices might also be incorrect.

   • If two of the choices are pretty much the same, both are probably wrong.

   • Answers that contain any of the following words are usually incorrect: *always, never, none, all,* and *only.*

5. If you're still unsure about an answer, see if any of the following applies:

   • When one choice is longer and more detailed than the others, it is often the correct answer.

   • When a choice repeats a word that is in the question, it may be the correct answer.

   • When two choices are direct opposites, one of them is likely the correct answer.

   • When one choice includes one or more of the other choices, it is often the correct answer.

   • When a choice includes the word *some* or *often*, it may be the correct answer.

   • If one of the choices is *All of the above*, make sure that at least two of the other choices seem correct.

   • If one of the choices is *None of the above*, make sure that none of the other choices seems correct.

An **open-ended test item** can take many forms. It might ask you

☑ **Reading Check** What words in a multiple-choice question probably signal a wrong answer?

to write a word or phrase to complete a sentence. You might be asked to create a chart, draw a map, or fill in a graphic organizer. Sometimes, you will be asked to write one or more paragraphs in response to a writing prompt. Use the following strategies when reading and answering open-ended items:

1. If the item includes directions, read them carefully. Take note of any steps required.

2. Look for key words and phrases in the item as you plan how you will respond. Does the item ask you to identify a cause-and-effect relationship or to compare and contrast two or more things? Are you supposed to provide a sequence of events or make a generalization? Does the item ask you to write an essay in which you state your point of view and then try to persuade others that your view is correct?

3. If you're going to be writing a paragraph or more, plan your answer. Jot down notes and a brief outline of what you want to say before you begin writing.

4. Focus your answer. Don't include everything you can think of, but be sure to include everything the item asks for.

5. If you're creating a chart or drawing a map, make sure your work is as clear as possible.

☑ **Reading Check** What are at least three key strategies for answering an open-ended question?

Reading Test Model
LONG SELECTIONS

DIRECTIONS Read the following excerpt from an article on the Atacama Desert. The notes in the side columns will help you prepare for the types of questions that are likely to follow a reading like this. You might want to preview the questions on pages 187 and 188 before you begin reading.

READING STRATEGIES FOR ASSESSMENT

Find the main idea. After reading the first two paragraphs, write down what you think this excerpt will be about.

Notice supporting details. The writer says that the Atacama has been called the driest place on Earth. What details does the author provide to support that statement?

Infer meaning from context clues. What does the word *arid* mean?

Dry, Drier, Driest

The golfer lines up his putt carefully on the green of the 7th hole at *El Club de Golf* near Arica on the Chilean coast. He strikes the ball solidly and sinks the putt to a smattering of applause from his golfing buddies. *El Club de Golf*, however, is no ordinary golf course. There is not a single blade of grass to be seen. The "greens" are actually hard rock spread with used motor oil. And the water hazards? Rock as well, painted blue.

Why? Because *El Club de Golf* is located in the Atacama Desert. The desert is about 600 miles long, stretching from southern Peru into northern Chile, and it has been called the driest place on Earth. The Atacama is so dry, in fact, that in some places no rainfall has ever been recorded for as long as humans have measured such things. In other places, such as the town of Antofagasta on the Pacific coast, heavy rains fall only a couple of times every *century!*

The arid climate of the Atacama can be traced to several meteorological phenomena. First, a permanent cell of high pressure over the Pacific Ocean prevents any storms from moving in from west of the desert. In the east, the Andes drain the moisture from clouds that have formed in the Amazon Basin. Finally, the cold waters of the Peru Current that flows up the coastline from Antarctica create a thermal inversion—cold air at the water's surface and warmer air above—that results in fog but no rain.

Still, the Atacama is not a lifeless place. When the atmospheric conditions are right, a dense fog called *camanchaca* develops along the coastline. The fog is just wet enough to sustain life on the cliffs high above the shore. There, shrubs and moss-covered cacti thrive along with gray foxes and rodents like the visacha, a relative of the chinchilla.

Despite the harsh conditions that plague the Atacama, the desert has been critical to the economic success of Chile for the past two centuries. During the 19th and early 20th centuries, sodium nitrate mining enriched the country. In fact, sodium nitrate was so highly prized that Chile, Bolivia, and Peru went to war over it. The War of the Pacific lasted from 1879 to 1883. At the war's end, the Treaty of Ancón gave Chile permanent possession of the sodium nitrate-rich lands previously controlled by Peru and Bolivia. Bolivia actually lost its entire Pacific coastline as a result of the war.

By the 1930s, the development of artificial nitrates spelled doom for Chile's nitrate mining industry. The Atacama, however, proved to be rich in other natural resources. Today, miners draw copper, silver, gold, and

Look for cause-and-effect relationships. List the three causes of the Atacama's dry climate.

Make predictions. How might Bolivia have been affected by the loss of its entire Pacific coastline?

Analyze visuals. Read the chart
carefully. What conclusions can
you draw about the size of the
Atacama?

_____

_____

_____

_____

Draw conclusions. Why do you
think the conditions mentioned
are ideal for star gazing?

_____

_____

_____

_____

_____

_____

_____

_____

_____

_____

_____

_____

_____

iron from the parched desert land. The Atacama has also become a tourist destination. So-called ecotourists—travelers interested in visiting the planet's most fascinating natural wonders—have contributed to an economic boom in the desert's three largest coastal cities.

Science has also benefited from conditions in the Atacama. The air is perfectly dry and perfectly clear. A sparse population means few lights. These are ideal circumstances for observing the heavens. That is why a group of European nations selected the Atacama as the location for the world's largest optical observatory. Located at Cerro Paranal, at an altitude of nearly 8,700 feet, the aptly named Very Large Telescope (VLT) peers deeply into the inky blackness of space. The VLT is actually four telescopes working in concert to produce the sharpest images of any observatory on Earth.

How Big Is the Atacama?

Desert	Location	Approximate Size, Sq. mi.
Death Valley	SW United States	3,000
Negev	S. Israel	4,700
Atacama	N. Chile	70,000
Gobi	Mongolia; China	500,000
Arabian	Arabian Peninsula	900,000
Sahara	N. Africa	3,500,000

Source: *The New York Times Almanac,* 2003

Now answer questions 1–6. Base your answers on the excerpt from "Dry, Drier, Driest." Then check yourself by reading through the Answer Strategies in the side columns.

1 Which of the following best describes the main idea of the excerpt?

A. The Atacama is economically important to Chile.

B. The Atacama is rich in mineral deposits.

C. The Atacama has perhaps the driest climate on Earth.

D. The Atacama has become a popular tourist destination.

> **Recall the main idea.** All four answer choices mention the Atacama. Only one answer choice, however, echoes the title of the article.

2 Which of the following is a synonym for *arid*?

A. moist

B. parched

C. humid

D. soggy

> **Think about context.** Three of these answer choices suggest moisture. The context of *arid*, however, is all about dryness.

3 Which of the following is NOT a cause of the Atacama's dry climate?

A. high-pressure cell

B. thermal inversion

C. Andes

D. El Niño

> **Pay attention to topic sentences.** The topic sentence of the third paragraph promises to tell the reader why the Atacama is so dry. Which answer choice is not included in that paragraph?

Answers:
1. C, 2. B, 3. D

4 Which desert is about seven times as large as the Atacama?

A. Gobi

B. Sahara

C. Negev

D. Death Valley

5 Which of the following describes a likely result of Bolivia losing its entire Pacific coastline?

A. increased economic prosperity

B. increased trade by sea

C. loss of port facilities

D. loss of rich farmland

6 Explain why the conditions in the Atacama are ideal for observing the heavens.

Sample short response for question 6:

The Atacama is ideal for observing the heavens because the atmosphere above it contains nothing that would interfere with the light coming from distant stars and planets. The atmosphere contains no droplets of moisture because of the dry climate. The atmosphere also contains no dust because the desert is sparsely populated. This means light comes through the atmosphere undistorted. Also, because the Atacama has so few people, there are very few lights to brighten the atmosphere. This leaves the sky absolutely black, which makes finding and observing objects in space much easier.

Answers:
4. A, 5. C

Reading Test Practice
LONG SELECTIONS

DIRECTIONS Now it's time to practice what you've learned about reading test items and choosing the best answers. Read the following selection, "The History and Artistry of Flamenco." Use the side columns to make notes about the important parts of this selection: important ideas, comparisons and contrasts, difficult vocabulary, interesting details, and so on.

The History and Artistry of Flamenco

Throughout its long history, Spain has contributed much to the world's art, architecture, literature, theater, and music. Spain's rich cultural heritage includes the paintings of Francisco de Goya, Pablo Picasso, and Salvador Dalí; the architecture of Antonio Gaudí; the literature of Miguel de Cervantes and Federico García Lorca; and music from the cello of Pablo Casals and the guitar of Andrés Segovia. Among these treasures is a haunting and complex art form whose roots are centuries old and a continent away—flamenco. Flamenco is best known throughout the world as a dance, but it is actually a trio of art forms: songs, dances, and musicianship.

Flamenco's Uncertain Origins The complete history of flamenco may never be fully known, but many music historians believe flamenco can be traced back to the Roma (Gypsy) people of Rajasthan in northwest India. From the 9th through the 14th centuries, the Roma migrated to Spain, bringing with them their musical traditions. These included songs, dances, and such musical instruments as tambourines, bells, and castanets—hand-held percussion instruments made of wood that produce a clicking sound. In Spain, the culture of the Roma mixed with that of Spain's Moors and Sephardic Jews. One of the results of that cultural blending was flamenco. Perhaps the best clue to the origins of flamenco can be found in a flamenco dance called the *baile grande*, or "profound dance." The hand, arm, and foot movements of this dance are remarkably similar to those of a classical dance performed by Hindus on the Indian subcontinent.

Beginnings in Song Interestingly, the heart of flamenco is the *cante*, or song. Some of these *cantes* have their roots in Spanish folk songs. Others have been influenced by Arab music. As flamenco continued to develop, Latin American music was added to the mix.

Generally, flamenco songs fall into one of three categories. First is the *cante jondo*, or "profound song." These songs are strongly emotional, taking as their subject matter such issues as death, despair, doubt, and anguish. The *cante intermedio*, or "intermediate song," is a second type of flamenco song. Also known as the *cante flamenco*, this song is a mixture of Spanish musical styles. Finally, there is the *cante chico*, or "light song." As the name implies, these songs are often humorous and deal with less emotional subjects than the *cante jondo*.

By the middle of the 1800s, flamenco songs were usually accompanied by guitar music. To keep the beat, a percussion instrument called a *palo seco*, or "dry stick," was beaten on the floor.

The Emergence of Dance After the mid-19th century, *baile*, or dance, became the most important component of flamenco. The male dancer, the *bailaor*, and the female dancer, the *bailaora*, were the actors in a flamenco performance, interpreting with their movements the story being sung by the singer, the *cantaor*.

Several parts of the body are emphasized in flamenco dancing: the arms, the upper torso, the hands, and the feet. Female dancers usually emphasize their hands and upper torsos, often using castanets to accent the rhythm of their body movements. In contrast, male dancers display elaborate footwork, punctuating their movements with the staccato sound of their boots slamming against the floor.

So intense is the flamenco dance that many dancers are believed to fall into a trancelike state called *duende*. This trance is fed by the clapping and shouting of the audience.

Flamenco Enters the 20th Century
During the last half of the 19th century, cafés dedicated to showcasing flamenco singing and dancing opened throughout Spain. As

flamenco dancing became more popular and widespread, however, many of its classic elements were de-emphasized in favor of a more dramatic, crowd-pleasing approach. To rescue flamenco in its original form, the poet and playwright Federico García Lorca and the composer Manuel de Falla staged the first flamenco competition in 1922. They stipulated that the performers had to offer authentic flamenco, not the new form that was popular in the cafés. The competition helped remind people of the origins of the art form.

Today, flamenco continues to evolve. Contemporary artists write new music and choreograph new dances, mindful of flamenco's centuries of tradition. In this way, one of Spain's oldest art forms is refreshed for new audiences to appreciate.

Now answer questions 1–6. Base your answers on the selection "The History and Artistry of Flamenco."

1 What is the author's purpose in this article?

   A. to persuade the reader that flamenco originated in India

   B. to describe the origins and techniques of flamenco

   C. to inform readers about the Roma migration

   D. to explain how flamenco compares with other elements of Spain's cultural heritage

2 Which of the following does NOT help explain the origins of flamenco?

   A. the Roma migration from India

   B. the mixing of Jewish, Moorish, and Roma culture

   C. the influence of Latin American music

   D. the similarities between a flamenco dance and an ancient Hindu dance

3 Which of the following names the flamenco song that deals with death, anguish, doubt, and despair?

   A. *cante jondo*

   B. *cante flamenco*

   C. *cante chico*

   D. *cante intermedio*

4 Which of the following does NOT contribute to the trancelike state called *duende*?

A. the intensity of the dance

B. the shouting of the audience

C. the clapping of the audience

D. the costume of the dancer

5 What contributed to the decline of the flamenco art form in the latter half of the 19th century?

A. small audiences

B. the growth of flamenco cafés

C. the influence of Latin American music

D. flamenco competitions

6 Explain the purpose of the flamenco competition of 1922.

THINKING IT THROUGH

The notes in the side columns will help you think through your answers. See the answer key at the bottom of this page and the next page. How well did you do?

1 What is the author's purpose in this article?

   A. to persuade the reader that flamenco originated in India

   B. to describe the origins and techniques of flamenco

   C. to inform readers about the Roma migration

   D. to explain how flamenco compares with other elements of Spain's cultural heritage

> Read the title of the article, which is often a clue to the author's purpose. Which answer choice best describes what the title promises?

2 Which of the following does NOT help explain the origins of flamenco?

   A. the Roma migration from India

   B. the mixing of Jewish, Moorish, and Roma culture

   C. the influence of Latin American music

   D. the similarities between a flamenco dance and an ancient Hindu dance

> The details about the origins of flamenco are contained in the second paragraph. Which answer choice contains information that is not in the second paragraph?

3 Which of the following names the flamenco song that deals with death, anguish, doubt, and despair?

   A. *cante jondo*

   B. *cante flamenco*

   C. *cante chico*

   D. *cante intermedio*

> When faced with a series of foreign words, their translations, and their definitions, it's important to read through them slowly and methodically. If you skim too quickly, you may wind up selecting an incorrect answer.

Answers: 1.B, 2.C, 3.A

Read the paragraph about *duende*. One of the answer choices contains a word that is not mentioned in the paragraph—a clue that this is the correct answer.

4 Which of the following does NOT contribute to the trancelike state called *duende*?

A. the intensity of the dance

B. the shouting of the audience

C. the clapping of the audience

D. the costume of the dancer

Pay attention to cause-and-effect relationships. What effect is mentioned in question 5? Where will you find the true cause?

5 What contributed to the decline of the flamenco art form in the latter half of the 19th century?

A. small audiences

B. the growth of flamenco cafés

C. the influence of Latin American music

D. flamenco competitions

This response received a top score because it
- provides the information the question asks for
- includes details from the passage
- is written clearly and has logical organization

6 Explain the purpose of the flamenco competition of 1922.

In 1922, Lorca and de Falla came to the conclusion that the classic flamenco was no longer being performed. In the popular flamenco cafés, the style of flamenco had been changed to make it more dramatic and pleasing to the crowds. Anyone participating in the flamenco competition had to perform authentic flamenco. In this way, Lorca and de Falla hoped to preserve the original art form.

Answers:
4. D, 5. B

Reading Test Model
SHORT SELECTIONS

DIRECTIONS The strategies you have just learned can also help you with this shorter selection, "Tikal." As you read the selection, respond to the notes in the side column.

When you've finished reading, answer the multiple-choice questions. Use the side-column notes to help you understand what each question is asking and why each answer is correct.

Tikal

In the lush tropical rain forest of northern Guatemala lie the ruins of the Maya city of Tikal, the ceremonial center of the ancient Maya civilization. Tikal got its start as a small village during the Middle Formative Period (900–300 B.C.) of Maya civilization. By the Late Formative Period (300 B.C.–A.D. 100), great temples and pyramids signified that the city had become an important ceremonial center.

Ceremony, however, was not the only role Tikal would play in Maya civilization. During the Early Classical Period (A.D. 100–600), Tikal was an important city in a vast trading network that included the central Mexican city of Teotihuacán. By the start of the Late Classical Period (A.D. 600–900), Tikal was a flourishing metropolis with an urban population of 10,000 inhabitants and an outlying population of around 50,000 people. Impressive plazas, palaces, and pyramids filled the city. During this same period,

READING STRATEGIES FOR ASSESSMENT

Note the periods of Maya civilization and their dates. How do these dates help you understand the development of Tikal?

Pay attention to topic sentences. What new information will this paragraph tell you about Tikal?

Find explanatory details. What information supports the topic sentence of the last paragraph?

_____

_____

_____

_____

_____

_____

Maya hieroglyphic writing appeared, as did a complex system for counting time. The citizens of Tikal created large sculptures and beautiful ceramics.

Around A.D. 800, Tikal began to decline. The population shrank, and the quality of Mayan artistry deteriorated. By the 10th century, the once-great city had been abandoned. Today, the ruins of Tikal lie in Tikal National Park. In 1979, the ruins were designated a UNESCO World Heritage site.

ANSWER STRATEGIES

Read the answer choices closely. The word *formative* indicates something being formed, like a city. Also, chances are a city would not be getting its start during a "late" period.

1 During which period of Maya civilization did Tikal get its start?

A. Late Formative

B. Late Classical

C. Early Classical

D. Middle Formative

Look for key words and phrases. The key phrase in the question is "Late Classical." The key phrase in the answer choices is "first appearance." What is contradictory about these two phrases?

2 Which of the following did NOT occur during the Late Classical Period?

A. the first appearance of great temples

B. the creation of large sculptures

C. the appearance of Maya hieroglyphic writing

D. the development of a complex system for counting time

Make intelligent assumptions. The first three answer choices here suggest a thriving civilization in a growing city. Only the final choice offers negative information.

3 Which of the following helps explain the decline of Tikal?

A. the building of impressive palaces

B. the appearance of hieroglyphic writing

C. participation in a vast trading network

D. decreasing population

Answers:
1. D, 2. A, 3. D

DIRECTIONS Some test questions ask you to analyze a visual rather than a reading selection. Study this chart carefully and answer the questions that follow.

Climate of Selected Latin American Cities

City	January			July		
	Temp. Max.	Min.	Avg. Precip.	Temp. Max.	Min.	Avg. Precip.
Bogotá, Colombia	67°	48°	2.3"	64°	50°	2.0"
Buenos Aires, Argentina	85°	63°	3.1"	57°	42°	2.2"
Caracas, Venezuela	75°	56°	0.9"	78°	61°	4.3"
Lima, Peru	82°	66°	0.1"	67°	57°	0.3"
Santiago, Chile	85°	53°	0.1"	59°	37°	3.0"

Temperatures given in degrees Fahrenheit.
Precipitation is average monthly amount in equivalent rainfall.

Source: *The New York Times Almanac,* 2003

4 Which city has the driest climate in both January and July?

A. Lima

B. Santiago

C. Caracas

D. Bogotá

5 Which city's maximum temperature varies the most between January and July?

A. Santiago

B. Caracas

C. Lima

D. Buenos Aires

6 Which city has the coldest temperature?

A. Bogotá

B. Santiago

C. Lima

D. Buenos Aires

READING STRATEGIES FOR ASSESSMENT

Read the title. What does the title tell you the chart is about?

_____

_____

_____

Read the key. How does the key help you understand the numbers in the chart?

_____

_____

_____

_____

ANSWER STRATEGIES

Read the numbers for both months. Two cities are tied for driest climate in January. What happens in July?

Do the math. Simple subtraction will give you the correct answer to question 5.

Look for the lowest number. The question includes both months, so the lowest number on the chart will give you the correct answer.

Answers:
4. A, 5. D, 6. B

Reading Test Practice
SHORT SELECTIONS

DIRECTIONS Use the following to practice your skills. Read the selection carefully. Then answer the multiple-choice questions that follow.

The People's Ballet

In 1959, at the Pan-American Games in Chicago, spectators were treated to a spectacular performance of Mexican folk dances. The dance company they saw had just adopted a new name, Ballet Folklórico de México, but its roots stretched back to 1952, when a young dancer and choreographer at the Mexican Academy of Dance decided to start her own dance company.

Amalia Hernández had been dancing since she was eight years old. She trained with both classical and modern dance teachers but found that neither style of dance expressed what she was feeling inside. Amalia loved the traditional songs and dances of Mexico, and in 1952 she started a company with just eight dancers, Ballet Moderno de México, to bring those songs and dances to a wide audience.

After its triumph in Chicago, the Ballet Folklórico received the support of an important patron, Adolfo López Mateos, the then-president of Mexico. At his urging, the National Institute of Fine Arts scheduled a weekly performance of the dance company, which proved wildly popular. Soon, additional weekly performances were scheduled, and Amalia Hernández's dance company became one of Mexico's cultural treasures. Today, locals and tourists alike flock to Mexico City to delight in this colorful parade of Mexican folk dancing.

1 What is the main purpose of this selection?

A. to persuade readers that the Ballet Folklórico is the best dance company in Mexico

B. to describe the types of dances the company creates

C. to tell a story about the Ballet Folklórico

D. to inform readers about the founding and success of the Ballet Folklórico

2 Why did Amalia Hernández start her dance company?

A. so they could perform at the Pan-American Games in Chicago

B. to showcase the folk dances of Mexican culture

C. because the president of Mexico asked her to

D. because she was unhappy with her work at the Mexican Academy of Dance

DIRECTIONS Use the graph below to answer the questions that follow.

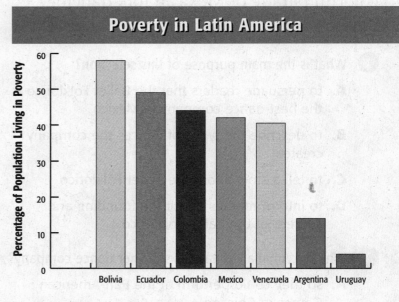

Poverty in Latin America

Percentage of Population Living in Poverty

Bolivia Ecuador Colombia Mexico Venezuela Argentina Uruguay

Source: *Social Panorama of Latin America,* 1998

3 What do the numbers on the left side of the graph represent?

A. the number of people living in poverty

B. the percentage of people living in poverty

C. the population of each country

D. the percentage of the total population of Latin America

4 In which country is the percentage of people living in poverty around three times the percentage in Uruguay?

A. Chile

B. Bolivia

C. Argentina

D. Venezuela

THINKING IT THROUGH

The notes in the side column will help you think through your answers. Check the key at the bottom of the page. How well did you do?

1 What is the main purpose of this selection?

A. to persuade readers that the Ballet Folklórico is the best dance company in Mexico

B. to describe the types of dances the company creates

C. to tell a story about the Ballet Folklórico

D. to inform readers about the founding and success of the Ballet Folklórico

> The first few words of each answer choice are key. This selection is informative, not descriptive or persuasive, and it doesn't tell a story.

2 Why did Amalia Hernández start her dance company?

A. so they could perform at the Pan-American Games in Chicago

B. to showcase the folk dances of Mexican culture

C. because the president of Mexico asked her to

D. because she was unhappy with her work at the Mexican Academy of Dance

> If you reread the selection carefully, you'll easily be able to eliminate all but the correct answer choice.

3 What do the numbers on the left side of the graph represent?

A. the number of people living in poverty

B. the percentage of people living in poverty

C. the population of each country

D. the percentage of the total population of Latin America

> Read all of the information in the graph carefully. One of the answer choices repeats the information almost word for word.

4 In which country is the percentage of people living in poverty around three times the percentage in Uruguay?

A. Chile

B. Bolivia

C. Argentina

D. Venezuela

> Look at the graph to determine Uruguay's percentage. Then, multiply that by three and check the graph again to find the country with that percentage.

Answers:
1. D, 2. B, 3. B, 4. C

Read the guide carefully. The steps are listed in chronological order. Notice that Step 4 offers two choices. If you select the second choice, you are presented with a list of options. Circle these options.

Interpret symbols. Circle each symbol in the guide. Be sure you understand what each symbol means.

Functional Reading Test Model

DIRECTIONS Study the following guide to storing contacts on a mobile phone. Then answer the questions that follow.

Storing Contacts on Your Mobile Phone

You can use the Contacts directory on your mobile phone to maintain information about an individual or a company. You should be able to store around 150 contacts. Just follow these five easy steps.

Entering and Storing a New Contact

1. Enter the phone number you want to store.
2. Press ⊚K to select **New Save.**
3. Enter the contact's name. For information on entering text in English or Spanish, see page 35.
4. Press ⊚K to select **Save.** Or press ⟨⟩ **Right** and then press ⊚K to select **Options.** Press ⟨⟩ **Up** or **Down** to select one of the following options:
   - **Save** This will save your information.
   - **Type of Number** This will identify the number as **work, home, fax, pager,** or **mobile.**
   - **Use Voice Recognition** Clearly say the name of the contact. This will enable you to dial the number using our exclusive voice recognition software.
   - **Speed Dial** You can select a speed dial code number from the list of available code numbers.
   - **Password Protected** If you select **yes,** the contact will be blocked from view. To view or edit the contact, you first have to enter your three-digit password.
5. Finally, press ⊚K to select **Save.** The message *Contact Saved!* will appear on the viewing screen.

1. How can you access the option that lets you use voice recognition?

A. Press Ⓞ🄺.

B. See page 35.

C. Press ⦿ **Right**, then press Ⓞ🄺 to select **Options**.

D. Enter your three-digit password.

The key word in this question is *option*. Which step includes options?

2. When must you use your three-digit password?

A. to view or edit a blocked contact

B. to speed dial a number

C. to save a new contact

D. to use voice recognition

The guide contains two special numbers: a password and a code number. Reread the guide to recall what each number enables you to do.

3. How can you speed dial a contact?

A. Enter the number and then press Ⓞ🄺.

B. Enter your three-digit password.

C. Press Ⓞ🄺 and select **Speed Dial**.

D. Assign a special code number to the contact.

Look through the guide for the boldface words **Speed Dial**. That is where you'll find the answer to question 3.

ANSWER STRATEGIES

Answers:
1. C, 2. A, 3. D

Functional Reading Test Practice

DIRECTIONS Study the following prescription label. Circle the information that you think is the most important. Then answer the multiple-choice questions that follow.

Ruiz Pharmacy
1700 West 19th Street
Chicago IL 60618
PH (773) 555-0168

Patient PH   (773) 555-7462

Alicia Delgado
3535 N. Summerdale
Chicago IL 60641

NO: 01448-78124
DATE: 8/26/03

Cozaar 50 mg tablets

TAKE ONE TABLET DAILY AT BREAKFAST

QTY: 30
REFILLS: 4

DR. M. del Valle

TAKE WITH FOOD

WARNING: Do not drive or operate heavy
machinery while taking this medication.

1. How long will this prescription last with refills?

   A. 1 month

   B. 5 months

   C. 2 months

   D. 6 months

2. How many milligrams of Cozaar must Señora Delgado take each day?

   A. 30 mg

   B. 4 mg

   C. 50 mg

   D. 40 mg

3. What must Señora Delgado do if she doesn't eat breakfast one day?

   A. skip the dose that day

   B. take the dose later in the day

   C. take the dose with food, perhaps a snack

   D. take two doses the next day

THINKING IT THROUGH

The notes in the side column will help you think through your answers. Check the answer key at the bottom of the page. How well did you do?

> Multiply the number of pills by the number of refills and add the original number of pills to determine how long the prescription will last.

1 How long will this prescription last with refills?

A. 1 month

B. 5 months

C. 2 months

D. 6 months

> Read the label carefully. Each pill is 50 mg, and the directions say to take one each day.

2 How many milligrams of Cozaar must Señora Delgado take each day?

A. 30 mg

B. 4 mg

C. 50 mg

D. 40 mg

> Each dose should be taken in the morning with food. It won't matter whether the dose is taken with breakfast or with a snack as long as it is taken in the morning.

3 What must Señora Delgado do if she doesn't eat breakfast one day?

A. skip the dose that day

B. take the dose later in the day

C. take the dose with food, perhaps a snack

D. take two doses the next day

Revising-and-Editing Test Model

DIRECTIONS Read the following paragraph carefully. Then answer the multiple-choice questions that follow. After answering the questions, read the material in the side columns to check your answer strategies.

[1]Last summer my cousins and me visited Mexico and we spent a morning in the city of Taxco. [2] We seen a brochure that said Taxco produced the best silverwork in the Western Hemisphere. [3]Even before the arrival of Columbus, the Native Americans were mining silver and other metals. [4]The Spanish became wealthy from the silver mines. [5]During the colonial period. [6]Because of its history and architecture, Mexico declared Taxco a national monument. [7]We would of stayed longer, but our bus was leaving for the return trip to Mexico City. [8]We plan to go there again one day. [9]We plan to explore the city further.

1 Which of the following is the best way to rewrite the beginning of sentence 1?

   A. Last summer, us cousins…

   B. Last summer, my cousins and I…

   C. Last summer, me and my cousins…

   D. Last summer, I and my cousins…

2 What is the correct way to punctuate the two complete thoughts in sentence 1?

   A. …visited Mexico: and we…

   B. …visited Mexico; and we…

   C. …visited Mexico, and we…

   D. …visited Mexico—and we…

ANSWER STRATEGIES

Personal Pronouns When deciding whether to use the personal pronoun *me* or *I* in a sentence, think about how the pronoun is used. If it's used as the subject, use *I*. If it's used as an object, use *me*.

Correct Punctuation Sentence 1 is a compound sentence. That is, it has two independent clauses joined by the conjunction *and*. In such cases, the correct punctuation is a comma.

Verb tense. Don't switch verb tenses. The verbs in sentences 1 and 3 are past tense, so the verb in sentence 2 should also be past tense.

3 Which of the following errors do you find in sentence 2?

A. incorrect verb tense

B. incorrect capitalization

C. unclear pronoun reference

D. misspelled word

Fragments. A complete sentence must have a subject and a verb and express a complete thought. Which sentence doesn't meet these requirements?

4 Which sentence in the paragraph is a fragment?

A. sentence 4

B. sentence 2

C. sentence 9

D. sentence 5

Correct verb usage. The word *of* is a preposition, not a verb. *Woulda* and *coulda* are not standard English.

5 Which of the following is the best way to rewrite the beginning of sentence 7?

A. We would have stayed longer…

B. We could of stayed longer…

C. We woulda stayed longer…

D. We coulda stayed longer…

Combining sentences. To avoid choppy writing, combine sentences with the same subjects and related information. If the new sentence contains an independent clause and a dependent clause, no punctuation is needed.

6 What is the best way to combine sentences 8 and 9?

A. We plan to go there again one day, and we plan to explore the city further.

B. We plan to go there again one day and explore the city further.

C. We plan to go there again one day; and we plan to explore the city further.

D. We plan to go there again one day, and explore the city further.

Answers:
1. B, 2. C, 3. A, 4. D, 5. A, 6. B

Revising-and-Editing Test Practice

DIRECTIONS Read the following paragraph carefully. As you read, circle each error that you find and identify the error in the side column—for example, *misspelled word* or *incorrect punctuation*. When you have finished, circle the letter of the correct choice for each question that follows.

¹ On August 2 1942 in Lima Peru, Isabel Allende was born. ² By the end of the 20th century, Allende was recognized as one of the most finest women novelists in all of Latin America. ³ Her first novel was published in 1982 it was called *La casa de los espíritus (The House of the Spirits).* ⁴ Many of Allendes novels focus on the role women play in Latin American society. ⁵ Like many Latin American novelists, Allende writes in a style called "magical realism." ⁶ The use of myths and fantasy in otherwise realistic works of fiction.

1 What is the correct way to punctuate the first part of sentence 1?

A. On August, 2, 1942 in Lima, Peru,

B. On August 2, 1942, in Lima, Peru,

C. On August 2, 1942, in Lima Peru,

D. On August 2 1942, in Lima, Peru,

2 Which of the following is the correct superlative to use in sentence 2?

A. finer

B. more finer

C. most finer

D. finest

3 Sentence 3 is a run-on. Which of the following is the best way to fix it?

A. Her first novel was published in 1982 and it was called *La casa de los espíritus (The House of the Spirits)*.

B. Her first novel was published in 1982. It was called *La casa de los espíritus (The House of the Spirits)*.

C. Her first novel was published in 1982: it was called *La casa de los espíritus (The House of the Spirits)*.

D. Her first novel was published in 1982; and it was called *La casa de los espíritus (The House of the Spirits)*.

4 Which resource would you consult to find a more interesting word for *called* in sentence 3?

A. dictionary

B. glossary

C. encyclopedia

D. thesaurus

5 Which of the following is the correct singular possessive form for *Allende* in sentence 4?

A. Allende's

B. Allendes'

C. Allendes's

D. Allendess'

6 Which sentence in the paragraph is a fragment?

A. sentence 4

B. sentence 6

C. sentence 5

D. sentence 1

THINKING IT THROUGH

Use the notes in the side columns to help you understand why some answers are correct and others are not. Check the answer key on the next page. How well did you do?

1 What is the correct way to punctuate the first part of sentence 1?

- **A.** On August, 2, 1942 in Lima, Peru,
- **B.** On August 2, 1942, in Lima, Peru,
- **C.** On August 2, 1942, in Lima Peru,
- **D.** On August 2 1942, in Lima, Peru,

> When writing dates, the day and the year are separated by commas and the year is separated from the rest of the sentence by a comma. When writing a place name, the city is separated from the country by a comma, and the country is separated from the rest of the sentence by a comma.

2 Which of the following is the correct superlative to use in sentence 2?

- **A.** finer
- **B.** more finer
- **C.** most finer
- **D.** finest

> The superlative form of an adjective or adverb can be formed in two ways. Either the word ends in *-est*, or the word is preceded by *most*. *Most* and the *-est* ending are never used together.

3 Sentence 3 is a run-on. Which of the following is the best way to fix it?

- **A.** Her first novel was published in 1982 and it was called *La casa de los espíritus (The House of the Spirits)*.
- **B.** Her first novel was published in 1982. It was called *La casa de los espíritus (The House of the Spirits)*.
- **C.** Her first novel was published in 1982: it was called *La casa de los espíritus (The House of the Spirits)*.
- **D.** Her first novel was published in 1982; and it was called *La casa de los espíritus (The House of the Spirits)*.

> The best way to fix this run-on sentence is just to divide it into two simple sentences.

4 Which resource would you consult to find a more interesting word for *called* in sentence 3?

A. dictionary

B. glossary

C. encyclopedia

D. thesaurus

5 Which of the following is the correct singular possessive form for *Allende* in sentence 4?

A. Allende's

B. Allendes'

C. Allendes's

D. Allendess'

6 Which sentence in the paragraph is a fragment?

A. sentence 4

B. sentence 6

C. sentence 5

D. sentence 1

Answers:
1. B, 2. D, 3. B, 4. D, 5. A, 6. B

Writing Test Model

DIRECTIONS Many tests ask you to write an essay in response to a writing prompt. A writing prompt is a brief statement that describes a writing situation. Some writing prompts ask you to explain *what, why,* or *how.* Others ask you to convince someone of something.

As you analyze the following writing prompts, read and respond to the notes in the side columns. Then look at the response to each prompt. The notes in the side columns will help you understand why each response is considered strong.

Prompt A

Everyone enjoys leisure time and everyone has a favorite way to enjoy such time. Think about what you like to do most with your leisure time.

Now write an essay that describes your favorite leisure activity. Include details that enable readers to understand and experience your enthusiasm.

Strong Response

Between school and working at my family's hardware store, I don't have much time to myself. However, when I can grab a couple of hours of free time, I love jumping on my bike and riding the back roads just outside of Carpentersville. Whether I'm alone or with friends, a long ride helps clear my mind and refresh my spirit.

I ride a road bike, a lightweight, sleek machine with a red pearl finish. Its drop handlebars, thin tires, and sixteen gears are perfect for propelling me along the gently rolling hills of these parts. I've devised several different routes through the countryside. Some are designed for speed—perfect for those days when I'm looking for a really good workout. Other routes are more scenic. I can take these

ANALYZING THE PROMPT

Identify the topic. Read the first paragraph of the prompt carefully. Underline the topic of the essay you will write.

Understand what's expected of you. The second paragraph of the prompt explains what you must do and offers suggestions on how to create a successful response.

ANSWER STRATEGIES

Grab the reader's attention. This opening paragraph is an invitation to the reader to go riding with the writer and experience what he experiences on his bike.

Provide interesting information. Here the writer describes his bike and the routes he takes, painting a picture for the reader.

at a slower pace and often choose them when I've got some thinking to do or when I just want to enjoy a beautiful day.

I also like the rituals of bike riding. I'm always tinkering with my bike, lubricating the gearing, adjusting the brakes, and making sure everything is screwed together tightly. Then there's the clothing: padded bike shorts, brightly colored jersey, leather-and-gel riding gloves, special shoes that attach securely to the pedals, and an aerodynamic helmet that matches the bike's finish. Sometimes I feel like an astronaut suiting up for a shuttle launch. Finally there are the accessories. I always carry a repair kit in case of breakdowns, a mini-pump for flat tires, and a medical kit in case of spills. My favorite accessory, though, is my trip computer. It tells me how fast I'm traveling and how far I've gone. It even monitors my heart rate!

Some of my friends think I'm a little obsessed with bike riding. Maybe they're right. But when I'm zooming down a long hill or leaning into a soft curve, feeling the wind rushing past, I experience a kind of joy and contentment that I can't get from anything else.

Prompt B

Since the mid-1990s, federal law has required television manufacturers to install a so-called "v-chip" in every television they produce. The v-chip allows the user to block certain channels unless a password is entered. The purpose of the v-chip legislation was to give parents control over what their children could access on television, whether the parents were present or not.

Think about the purpose of the v-chip. Do you agree or disagree with the law that made it mandatory? Is it useful technology for parents, or does it unfairly limit what children can watch? Write an essay in which you state your opinion and provide convincing arguments to support that opinion.

Strong Response

My family recently installed a satellite dish on the roof of our house. We now have access to over 200 television channels. Most of the programming on these channels is harmless: cartoons, sitcoms, sports, cooking, home improvement, and so on. Some of the channels, however, present programming that is suitable only for adults. I believe the government was right to insist that television manufacturers install v-chip technology so that parents can block unwanted programming if they choose to.

I am sixteen years old, and my younger sisters are eight and twelve years old. Our parents try to pay close attention to what we watch on television, but that's not always possible. For example, when my parents go out for the evening and I'm at home taking care

ANALYZING THE PROMPT

Identify the topic. The first paragraph of the prompt makes it clear that the topic is v-chip technology.

Know what's expected of you. The second paragraph of the prompt lets you know that you're going to write an essay in which you take a position and provide arguments to support that position.

ANSWER STRATEGIES

Engage the reader's interest. The writer begins on a personal note to draw the reader into the essay.

State the position clearly. The last sentence of the introductory paragraph states the writer's position clearly and forcefully.

Begin supporting the position. The writer begins supporting her position by acknowledging that even well-intentioned parents can't be everywhere.

of my sisters, there are no adults to supervise what we watch on tv.

Sometimes, unsuitable programming can show up on the screen even when you're not looking for it. You might be channel surfing with no particular program in mind and suddenly stumble across a program clearly intended for adults. Until the government acted, there was nothing parents could do about such accidental discoveries.

With v-chip technology, however, parents can take action. Using simple, on-screen prompts, parents can block access to any channels they don't want their children to see. These channels might present adult programming, excessively violent programming, movies that may be suitable for some children but not for others, and so on.

My parents told me when our dish was being installed that they intended to block a number of channels they felt were not suitable for our family. At first I thought that was unfair, but the more I thought about it, the more I realized my parents were just doing their job as parents. I don't know how many channels they blocked, and I don't really care. We've still got about 175 channels to watch, and that's plenty for any family.

Use language that echoes the prompt. The phrase "until the government acted" reminds readers of the topic introduced in the prompt.

Expand the argument. The writer adds to her argument by noting that adult programming is just one type of programming that parents might find offensive or unsuitable.

Acknowledge other points of view. The writer admits that at first she was against the idea of blocking channels but now understands why parents find this technology useful.

Writing Test Practice

DIRECTIONS Read the following writing prompt. Using the strategies you've learned in this section, analyze the prompt, plan your response, and then write an essay explaining your position.

Prompt C

Due to a serious budget crisis, your school district must find ways to save money. The school board has decided to lay off some teachers and increase the number of students in each class by five to ten students.

Think about the effect additional students in each class will have on students and teachers. Has the school board made a sound decision in your opinion? Write a letter to the board that explains why you favor or oppose their decision. State your position clearly and provide persuasive supporting arguments.

Scoring Rubrics

DIRECTIONS Use the following checklist to see whether you have written a strong persuasive essay. You will have succeeded if you can check nearly all of the items.

The Prompt

☐ My response meets all the requirements stated in the prompt.

☐ I have stated my position clearly and supported it with details.

☐ I have addressed the audience appropriately.

☐ My essay fits the type of writing suggested in the prompt (letter to the editor, article for the school paper, and so on).

Reasons

☐ The reasons I offer really support my position.

☐ My audience will find the reasons convincing.

☐ I have stated my reasons clearly.

☐ I have given at least three reasons.

☐ I have supported my reasons with sufficient facts, examples, quotations, and other details.

☐ I have presented and responded to opposing arguments.

☐ My reasoning is sound. I have avoided faulty logic.

Order and Arrangement

☐ I have included a strong introduction.

☐ I have included a strong conclusion.

☐ The reasons are arranged in a logical order.

Word Choice

☐ The language of my essay is appropriate for my audience.

☐ I have used precise, vivid words and persuasive language.

Fluency

☐ I have used sentences of varying lengths and structures.

☐ I have connected ideas with transitions and other devices.

☐ I have used correct spelling, punctuation, and grammar.

Apuntes

Apuntes

Apuntes

Apuntes

Apuntes

Apuntes

Credits

Illustrations

24–25 Lisa Henderling; **34–35** Gerardo Suzan.

All other illustrations by McDougal Littell/Houghton Mifflin Co.

Photography

4 *bottom* Michael & Patricia Fogden/Minden Pictures; *top* ZSSD/Minden Pictures; *center* HIRB/Index Stock Imagery; **8** Martin Rogers/Corbis; **9** Dan Milner/StockShot/Alamy; **13** *top* Carlo Fumagalli/AP Images; *bottom* right Risteski Goce/ShutterStock; *bottom* left ShutterStock; **14** *top* Allsport UK/Allsport/ Getty Images; *Uruguay flag* McDougal Littell/Houghton Mifflin Co.; *all other flags* ShutterStock; **18** *top* Diego Giudice/Corbis; *bottom* Corbis; **19** *right* José Miguel Gómez/Reuters; *left* Enzo & Paolo Ragazzini/Corbis; **29** *top* Suzanne Murphy-Larronde; *bottom left* Jorge Albán/McDougal Littell/ Houghton Mifflin Co.; *bottom right* Robert Fried/Alamy; **30** Kevin Schafer/Corbis; **39** *left* M. H. De León/Agencia EFE; *right* McDougal Littell/Houghton Mifflin Co.; **40** *bottom* CAMARI; *top* Owen Franken/Corbis; **44, 45** *decorative border* McDougal Littell/Houghton Mifflin Co.; **45** *right* PhotoDisc; *left* Michael Busselle/Corbis; **49** *left* Purple Marbles/Alamy; *right* Marie-Louise Avery/age fotostock; **50** *seafood* Kevin Sánchez/Cole Group/Getty Images; *street scene* Natacha Pisarenko/AP Images; **54, 55** *all Miramax Films;* **59** Ric Francis/AP Images; **60** *left inset* Guillermo Ogam//NewsCom/Notimex; *right* Morgana Alhen/NewsCom/Notimex; **64** *top* Jon Feingersh/zefa/Corbis; *bottom* Allan Penn/McDougal Littell/Houghton Mifflin Co.; *background* McDougal Littell/Houghton Mifflin Co.; **65** Allan Penn/ McDougal Littell/Houghton Mifflin Co.; **69** *Image 100*/age fotostock; **70** David Young-Wolff/PhotoEdit; **74** *left* Francois Gohier/Photo Researchers, Inc.; *right* Pablo Rugel/EMS/Zuma Press; **75** *right* Fasol M./Photo Researchers, Inc.; *center* Valerie Giles/Photo Researchers, Inc.; *left* Robert Frerck/Odyssey Productions, Inc.; **79** Diario Hoy; **80** *both* Yucef Merhi. **147** "Pope Alexander VI Borgia Kneeling in Prayer" *(detail)*, date unknown, Bernardino Pinturicchio. Sala die Mistera della Fede, Appartamento Borgia, Vatican Palace, Vatican State/Scala/Art Resource, New York; **157** Layne Kennedy/Corbis; **159** *green tea* Art Bank/Photonica, *yerba maté* © 2003 Robert Frerck/Odyssey Productions; **161** Geri Engberg/The Image Works; **163** The Granger Collection, New York.

All other photos by Lawrence Migdale/PIX/McDougal Littell/ Houghton Mifflin Co.